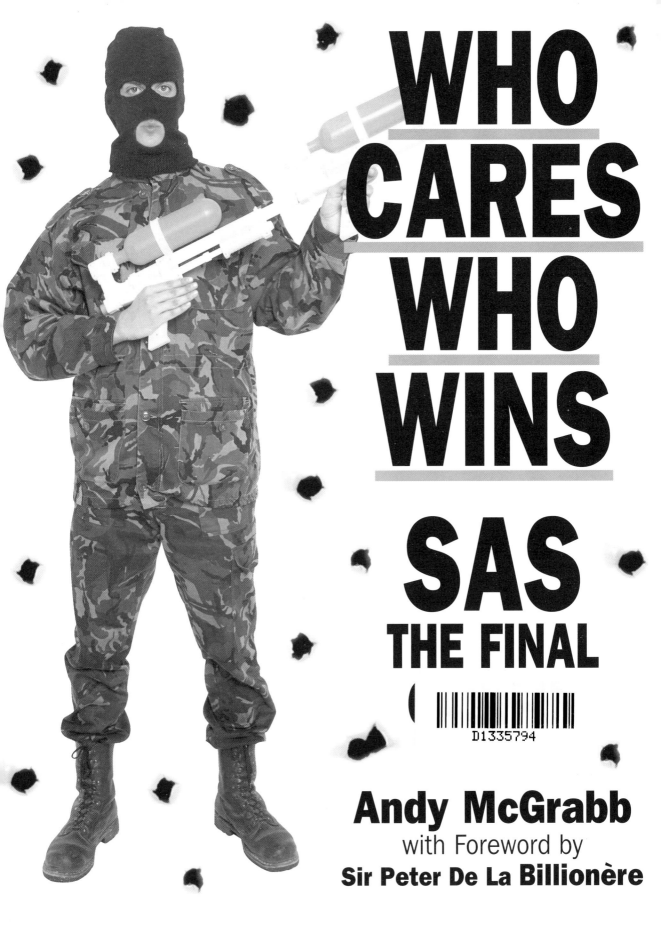

# WHO CARES WHO WINS

## SAS THE FINAL

D1335794

**Andy McGrabb**
with Foreword by
**Sir Peter De La Billionère**

First published in Great Britain in 1996 by
PAVILION BOOKS LIMITED
26 Upper Ground, London SE1 9PD

Special photography copyright © Julien Busselle

Designed and produced by ~~THE BRIDGEWATER BOOK COMPANY LIMITED~~

Art Direction: Field-Marshall ~~Terry~~ 'No. 5 Iron' ~~Jeavons~~
Design: Major ~~Glyn~~ 'Zippo' ~~Bridgewater~~
        Captain ~~John~~ 'Spartacus' ~~Christopher~~

A CIP catalogue record for this book is available from the
British Library

ISBN 1 85793 958 1

Bloody fast Repro by Anglia Graphics Ltd., Bedford

Printed and bound by Cambus Litho Ltd., East Kilbride

1 2 3 4 5 6 7 8 9 10

This book may be ordered by post direct from the publisher.
Please contact the Marketing Department.
But try your bookshop first.

From: HEAD SHED - General Sir Peter De La Billionère

To: Self

Re: Foreword: Who Cares Who Wins

Damn and blast. I hate doing these bloody things. Don't these people realise I'm a soldier, not a writer… Still, money for jam, I suppose and I can hardly leave such a delicate task to that semi-literate peasant McGrabb. I don't care how many books he's sold. You simply can't expect anyone who's not an officer to strike the right tone.

Right. To work. Tum tee tah. Oh look, there's a house martin hovering over the bird bath. Must remember to set the snare, or they'll all be in there before you can say Jack Frost.

Right. Concentrate. All that ghastly man from Pavilion wants is a hundred or so words extolling the supposed virtues of this opportunistic grab-bag of nonsense, which they're hoping to flog to the plebs as the definitive SAS volume. Idiots. Don't they realise I have already written that myself, viz 'Memo Two Zero – A Soldier's In-Tray'? By the way, wonder why it didn't sell more copies? Maybe that cover shot of a paper-clip was a mistake, after all.

Anyway, back to this tawdry money-making exercise. What have we got here? Who Cares Who Wins: The Final Cash-in. True stories behind top-secret missions. Extracts from the X Squadron training manual. Regimental histories, survival tips, handy hints on bringing SAS skills to real life? Well, I suppose someone will be interested, if they're staggering around drunk on Christmas Eve looking for something to give the brother-in-law.

Come on, got to say something positive about it. After all, it was my idea in the first place, and let's face it, old bean, if that last letter from Lloyd's was anything to go by, you need every last bean you can muster. I suppose the pictures are nice.

Come on, man, you're a highly trained professional. You've written hundreds of these forewords before. You even read some of the books first. Alright. I've got it.

'In over thirty years' distinguished service in the Regiment I have seen many SAS books. This is undoubtedly another one of them.'

That ought to do nicely. Right. Lunchtime, I suspect.

General Sir Peter De La Billionère

# X SQUADRON

## 22 SAS (AUXILIARY)

## ACKNOWLEDGEMENTS

Due to security measures, the true names of the authors cannot be revealed. However, Andy McGrabb of 29 Psoriasis Close, Herpes, Sussex (current Members of the SAS can find him in the 'Frog and Firefight', Hereford most nights) and General Sir Peter De La Billionère of 'Dunmerchandising' Long Meadow Retirement Villas, Harare (takes his Wednesday bath alfresco in the grounds of Government house at 7pm very near the conveniently placed incinerator) would like to thank a number of individuals for their support. Toby 'Water Pistol' Ashmore, Frank 'Warrior Class' Kaizik, Victoria 'Xerox' Webb, James 'Camping Gas' Walters and Dan 'The Man" Carboni whose bone duties on the cuds on hard routine ensured the MSR to publication. If you are unable to decipher the above you must either a) Read the glossary of pointless acronyms and slang at the back of the book; b) read the label on your medication again; c) enlist now.

## Terence McCracken

Born: _Milan   25/12/61

Rank:   I'm a very private person.

Nickname:   Mousse

Highlight of career: Too numerous to mention - London, Paris, New York, Munich...

Most dangerous opponent:  Stubborn unwanted nasal hair

Top tip for youngsters:  Whatever the temptation, never, ever put Immac up your nasal cavity.

If you weren't in the SAS:  Designing my own label.

Hero:  Nelson Mandela

## Harry Pryce

Born:   Fishguard Ferry Terminal

Rank:   Private

Nickname:   Side Salad

Highlight of career:  Managing to get back from Gulf War in time to honour reservation at The Waterside Inn.

Most dangerous opponent:   Keith Floyd

Top tip for youngsters: There's no such thing as too much garlic.

If you weren't in the SAS:  Sous chef

Hero:  Johnny Craddock

## Rupert D'eath-Cutie

Born:  Great Ormond Street

Rank:   Officer Material

Nickname:  Rupert

Highlight of career:  Runner-up for Sandhurst Sword of Honour.

Most dangerous opponent:  The working class

Top tip for youngsters:  Pass the port to the left.

If you weren't in the SAS:   Estate agent

Hero:  The Queen Mother

## Andy McGrabb

Born: Bethlehem. In a manger. Keep it under your hat.

Rank: Corporal (Catering)

Nickname: No Mates (a.k.a. No Sperm)

Highlight of career: Being badged.

Most dangerous opponent: My ex-wives - The Four Kimberleys

Top tip for youngsters: Don't marry women named after South African Provinces.

If you weren't in the SAS: Territorial Army

Hero: Mother

## Scud

Born: Holloway Prison

Rank: Pending appeal.

Nickname: See above.

Highlight of career: Headbutting 37 REMFS in under a minute. A Regimental record.

Most dangerous opponent: Yet to meet him.

Top tip for youngsters: Practice Makes Perfect

If you weren't in the SAS: Prison or selling cigarettes to the Africans.

Hero: Jimmy 'Five Bellies' Gardner

## Rabuka Kamisese Mara

Born: Fiji

Rank: Fijian

Nickname: Fiji Bob

Highlight of career: Being spoken to.

Most dangerous opponent: The language barrier

Top tip for youngsters: Don't.

If you weren't in the SAS: Back home in Fiji.

Hero: Va'aiga Tuigamala

X SQUADRON

# The Early Years — 1941

The 22 SAS Regiment was formed in the desert of North Africa over 50 years ago by David Stirling. A few weeks later, 22 SAS (Auxiliary) was formed by his batman's brother-in-law, Leonard Worsnip – a Streatham theatrical impresario drafted in 1940. Worsnip argued that the new elite fighting force would need a concert party. Due to a shortage of uniforms and the general heat of the desert base, Worsnip suggested a nude version of Homer's *Iliad* as the debut production.

When Stirling refused, citing some homoerotic undertones, Worsnip proposed a general auxiliary and reserve force that would 'mop up' after major operations and serve as a repository for all those 'promising young lads' who had failed training and selection 'by a whisker', as he put it. Stirling was unconvinced and told Worsnip in no uncertain terms to get out of his tent and stop bothering him. It was at this point that Worsnip produced the grenade and unbuttoned his tunic to reveal seventeen sticks of dynamite strapped to his vest.

Many of the skills learned during Stirling's ten-day ordeal as Worsnip's hostage served the regiment well in the Iranian Embassy siege and proved beyond doubt Worsnip's perspicacity and initiative. 22 SAS (Auxiliary) was founded on the day of Colonel Leonard Worsnip's tragic death by firing squad. His tombstone is inscribed with his last words, 'I've always loved you Private Benton. You may fire when ready.'

WORSNIP'S UNFORTUNATE BIRTHMARK SET THE TONE FOR ALL FUTURE PICTURES OF 22 SAS. THE BLACK BARS WORN ACROSS THE EYES OF THE REGIMENT SINCE ARE MEANT AS A TRIBUTE TO A GREAT SOLDIER AND HAVE LITTLE TO DO WITH MAINTAINING ANONYMITY.

FOUNDER OF 22 SAS (AUXILIARY) COLONEL LEONARD WORSNIP SHAKING HANDS WITH NEW RECRUITS ON THE DAY OF THE REGIMENT'S FORMATION.

# COMMAND STRUCTURE

| INVESTMENT PORTFOLIO MANAGER (ZURICH) | GENERAL SIR PETER DE LA BILLIONÈRE | SAS RETIREMENT FUND (LICHTENSTEIN) |

SQUADRON LEADER RUPERT D'EATH-CUTIE

| CHIEF RECONNAISSANCE OFFICER | TROOP COMMANDER CORPORAL ANDY McGRABB | QUARTERMASTER |

| PR, PRESS AND PUBLICITY | PUBLISHER | MARKETING |

| HAIR AND MAKE-UP | | LIBEL LAWYER |

| AROMATHERAPIST | LITERARY AGENT | COLONIC IRRIGATION |

| CATERING – 'LA PETITE ARMALITE' Phone for reservation | AUXILIARY SQUADRON (Soldiers) | MERCHANDISING T-shirts Novelty key rings |

*T*he squadron were all on edge, bored with the bone tasks laid out for us at Hereford. Since Dago Portillo's insistence that half the Regiment's costs should come from private finance, life at Hereford Barracks had changed. One Tuesday we were testing M & S corduroy trousers in a combat situation. Not a task we relished. Mousse didn't mind the double-pleated waistband but argued that taupe was an inappropriate shade for desert warfare.

**SAS Casual – A timeless style**

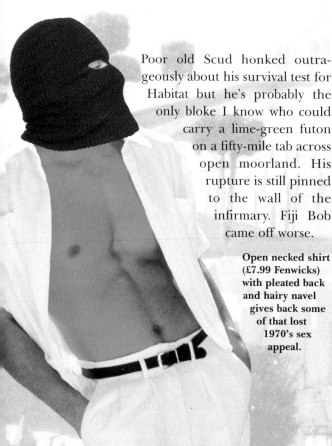

Poor old Scud honked outrageously about his survival test for Habitat but he's probably the only bloke I know who could carry a lime-green futon on a fifty-mile tab across open moorland. His rupture is still pinned to the wall of the infirmary. Fiji Bob came off worse.

**Open necked shirt (£7.99 Fenwicks) with pleated back and hairy navel gives back some of that lost 1970's sex appeal.**

The British Home Stores electric hibachi set was probably a step too far for a river crossing. Particularly after I plugged it in for him.

So it was dead chuffed we were when called to OPSEC for a briefing on a foreign covert op, code-named Rodent One, a joint infil with the French Foreign Legion. After the briefing we filed into the Hereford Hitachi Harvester Cafe and Patisserie and ordered a round of B & Q Cocktails and a couple of Sun Alliance Insurance croissants in honour of our new Frog colleague.

Our French CO was to be Commandant Jean Marc De Fortnum, a fine soldier but, like all the French, likely to compromise your soap-on-a-rope in a shower situation. He laid out the plan. In French. They just don't try, do they?

The target was a small kingdom. Some kind of rogue banana republic, backed by the Yanks, that was threatening the British and French way of life. They were taking over everything – cinemas, toy shops, childhood. They had to be stopped and we were just the crew to do it.

As I pushed Rupert out of the aircraft, I couldn't help feeling a surge of excitement which was uncomfortable in a parachute crotch harness. I felt like I was about to open a new packet of Hob Nobs – struggling with the wrapper, knowing the rewards are worth the hassle, then slipping the first unbroken disc from its shell and taking a bite out of destiny, leaving a trail of crumbs in history. It felt good.

We landed in some sort of local fortress and abseiled down past the stained-glass windows. There was a bird inside having a kip, but we didn't bother her. She wasn't the Head Shed in this situation. He would be making a personal appearance at 1300, according to the spooks, and we had to set up a good LUP before calling in.

We established a good line of surveillance in a maze next to a statue of some local VIP. A huge caterpillar smoking opium. Sick bastards. Scud spotted a secondary target torturing some kids outside the ice-cream parlour. They were being forced to sing a propaganda anthem. Their brainwashed little souls cried out for help and the sound rang in our ears like some Belgian entry in the Eurovision Song Contest. 'It's a small, small world...' It was chilling.

'Let me take him, Skip,' said Scud. 'He's on his own and he's only got a sailor hat.'

'It's too risky, mate,' I countered. 'There's a dog with him. Wait for the main target.'

We didn't have to wait long. We hit him just as he was posing for another photo opportunity with some Japanese tourists. Before anyone knew what was happening, we had him out of Main Street and tied to a chair in the centre of a huge maze. We knew there wasn't much time. Already an enemy contingent of munchkins were searching for us.

**Capacious trousers (£4.99 Tesco) for dangerous weaponry and the stripes are very slimming.**

My orders were simple: slot the target and exfil, blowing up any vital installations in our way. Fiji Bob had already placed shaped charges in Space Mountain, and Scud had been unable to resist wasting the feathered one with the webbed feet that we'd spotted earlier. I had to stop Scud skinning him for souvenirs and he was still shouting 'Send me the bill!' as I dragged him away.

The truth was, the lads were hyper. We'd lost a lot of good people to the pathetic creature tied to the chair, and his very existence was a threat to everything we held dear. I made a tough decision that I knew would shock those outside the Regiment. I decided to let the lads have a go at him before we did the deed. It was only fair.

Side Salad was first. He gave the target a good right-hander across the snout, dislodging a few whiskers. 'That's for making Winnie the Pooh sound like he's from Oklahoma,' he snarled. Mousse held a lighted match to the huge ears and watched them flare up like two huge fireballs. 'That's for letting Spielberg turn Peter Pan into a New York yuppie with a mobile phone.'

Rupert took the little monster's three-fingered hand and crushed it in a vice. 'That's for making my kids more comfortable cuddling a five-foot amphibious waterfowl with a speech impediment than me.'

I stopped myself from taking part and stood politely aside for our French guest. De Fortnum's people had suffered too. 'That's for the Hunchback of Notre Dame, *con de souris*. It's not supposed to have a happy ending,' he hissed as he sliced off the little black nose.

We all stood well back as I levelled the Sterling 9mm. 'That's for Dick Van Dyke.' They all nodded as his little body jerked and danced with lead.

We'd all shared puberty with Mary Poppins and it still hurt.

Scud was looking dead pensive as we boarded the chopper amid the blazing ruins of Fantasyland. 'I really wanted to ask him something,' he honked. 'What was it, mate?' I said. 'Why he did it? There's no rhyme or reason to the evil empire, Scud. The mouse does it because he wants power over everything. We can't get involved in politics. We're just here to do a job.'

'No,' replied Scud. 'That's not what I wanted to ask him.' 'What then?' exploded Mousse. Scud frowned and his little shaved head burned red with mental effort. 'If Mickey is a mouse and Pluto is a dog, what's Goofy?'

**After the operation the Regiment formally adopted this new headgear as part of its dress uniform.**

# Fiji Bob's Astrological Guide to the Fijian Zodiac

## ♈ THE FIJIAN ZODIAC

### Fiji Bob's STARS

### MacNabalam
**MAR 20–APRIL 18**

MACNABALAM is a fire sign. They should be fired upon as much as possible. Macnabalams are prone to indecision and may go to pieces when the chips are down. Humourless Saturn rising makes Macnabalams totally without irony and lacking in basic self-awareness. They have a tendency to rewrite history to suit themselves and may try to sell you film rights to a badly written memoir about a baby abandoned on the steps of a hospital, growing up to be an inarticulate cod philosopher who cocks up his job, his friends and his love life. They enjoy erotic weaponry, crying in supermarkets, fine ales and sunsets over water.

**THIS WEEK**
The full moon earlier this week will bring matters with loved ones out in the open, but only now do you realise what they are trying to say. 'Your books don't sell any more Andy. The SAS thing is played out. Call us again when you write a bonkbuster set in the Hereford Holiday Inn. Ciao.' Disputes with colleagues are also coming to a head and Wednesday will be turbulent with grenades under your bed making an unwelcome reappearance.

Lucky sandwich: Your own foot between two pieces of wholemeal bread
Lucky after shave: 'Eau d'Argent' par Macmillan

## ♈ THE FIJIAN ZODIAC ♎

### Fiji Bob's STARS

### Ryangalam
**DEC 21–JAN 19**

RYANGALAM, in the constellation of O'Ryan, is a water sign and may sometimes drink its own urine on long journeys. Ryangalams are confident, assured and a bit of a smart-arse. They are constantly saying 'I told you so' and 'It was Andy's fault'. The moon in their opposing sign of Macnabalam makes them moody and introspective particularly in the company of inferiors. They enjoy designer leatherwear, long walks and quiet evenings under the stars.

**THIS WEEK**
Mercury's difficult aspect to the stern planet Saturn could mean that you are in danger of becoming too perfect. Your infallibility and close facial resemblance to Robert Powell in *Jesus of Nazareth* may be more than your workmates can stand. Early in the week, you will survive a 300 mile trek, escape death by a whisker in an armed engagement and emerge from torture, exposure and starvation almost unscathed. Later in the week you will be run over by a milk float in the Edgware Road and die from your injuries. You will be resurrected over the weekend and will return to work on Monday refreshed and ready for new challenges.

Lucky sandwich: Sour pickle with vinegar dressing
Lucky after shave: Boots 'Man of Steel'

## ♈ THE FIJIAN ZODIAC ♎

# WHAT'S IN MY BERGEN?

## Scud

# Scud's Top Ten Insults

**I** don't care what anyone says, being able to engage in hand-to-hand honking (insulting banter) with other blokes is as big a part of a soldier's life in the Squadron as your personal fitness or being able to take on 400 towel-heads with one hand tied behind your back. In fact, in a mad, bad, dangerous world it's the only thing that keeps us all sane. Personally speaking I would never trust my life to anyone who doesn't call me a crap-headed wanker at least ten times a day. After all, what else are real friends for? (Don't answer that.) Here is my list of all-time Top Ten Devastating Insults.

**NB Use with caution. In the right circumstances, words can be more destructive than a home-made Claymore with 2lb of PE4.**

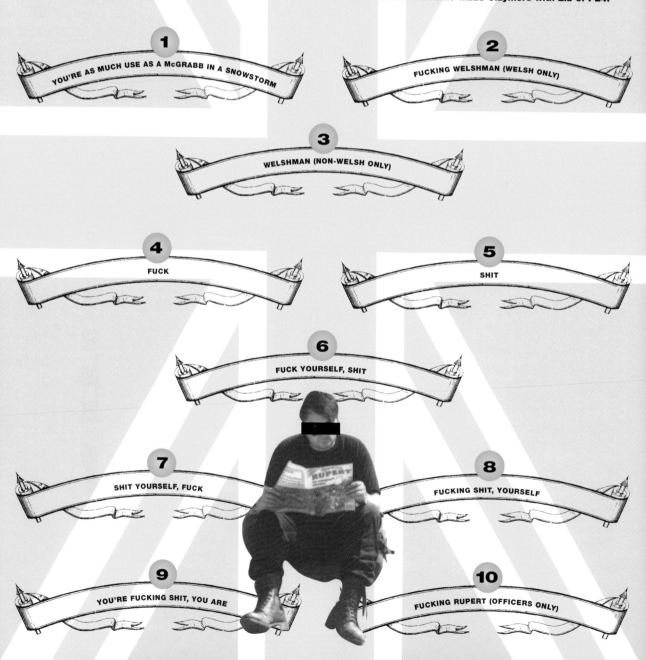

**1** YOU'RE AS MUCH USE AS A McGRABB IN A SNOWSTORM

**2** FUCKING WELSHMAN (WELSH ONLY)

**3** WELSHMAN (NON-WELSH ONLY)

**4** FUCK

**5** SHIT

**6** FUCK YOURSELF, SHIT

**7** SHIT YOURSELF, FUCK

**8** FUCKING SHIT, YOURSELF

**9** YOU'RE FUCKING SHIT, YOU ARE

**10** FUCKING RUPERT (OFFICERS ONLY)

# Special Air Service Selection Tests

## Part 1 Personal Details

1) Name:

2) Nickname:

3) Writing name:

4) Date of birth:

5) Place of birth:

(If unknown then state exactly where you were found and, if possible, what kind of plastic bag they found you in.)

6) Education:

7) Previous employment:

8) Criminal record:

**9) How did you hear about the SAS? (Tick as appropriate)**

a) Through a friend/colleague/cell mate ☐

b) Local radio/newspaper ads ☐

c) Best-selling SAS memoir ☐

   If so please state which one(s)

d) Film/TV tie-in ☐

e) Loud drunk bloke with a moustache shooting his mouth off in the local pub ☐

**10) Have you ever killed anybody?** ☐ Yes ☐ No

If your answer was 'Yes', then which band best represents the number of successful slottings:
1–5; 6–10; 11–15; 16–20; 20+; Can't remember, they were all foreigners.

11) Starsign:

12) Favourite band/singer:

13) Fave colour:

14) How long have you been a *Smash Hits* reader?

# Special Air Service Aptitude Tests

**Answer the following questions using a sharp HB pencil. Time allowed is one hour. Marks will be deducted for crossings-out, unnecessary flippancy and/or swearing in the margin.**

## Maths

1) Steve puts on a 120lb Bergen, leaves point A at 14.00 hrs and tabs 17 miles due east to point B where he rests for 11 mins 20 secs. Before he leaves he sheds 4.95 kilos of deadweight in a cache and notes the headwind is blowing at 57.6 mph due west. He tabs a further 59,000 furlongs south by south-west, using up 3,148 KJ of energy before he arrives at point C. What is his mother's maiden name?

2) Read the following royalty statement and answer the question below:

Freeman, Hardy & Willis – Literary Agents
Author's Statement: A. McGrabb, *The One Who Went Shopping*

| | |
|---|---:|
| Hardback sales: 79,546 @ 15.00p= | £11,931.90 |
| 675,000 copies @ 12.34p= | £83,295.00 |
| Book Club sales= | £43,715.70 |
| Sub total= | £138,942.60 |

If you were paying your agent commission at 10%, what is the statistical probability of you sleeping with his secretary?

## Geography

1) Oman is:
a) An oil-rich Arabic state friendly to Britain.  ☐
b) Something hippies say when they're stoned.  ☐
c) What they call wanking in the Bible.  ☐

2) Madras is:
a) A vibrant port city on the south-east coast of India.  ☐
b) The girly version of MaTrousers.  ☐
c) Not as hot as a Vindaloo obviously, but a darn sight less poofy than a Korma.  ☐

3) Which of the following statements do you agree with most? Wales is:
a) A proud Celtic nation with a viable future in Europe.  ☐
b) Closer than Scotland.  ☐
c) Fucked. The bloody Taffs can't even win at rugby these days.  ☐

## History and Politics

1) Who won the war but lost the penalty shoot-out? .............................................................

2) Spot the dictator.

**SADDAM HUSSEIN** ☐  **IDI AMIN** ☐  **DENG XIAOPING** ☐  **TONY BLAIR** ☐

3) List your top three battles and say why you enjoyed them. Factors to bear in mind include yardage gained, losses per minute and how pointless the whole thing was in the first place.

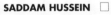

## English

1) One of Andy McGrabb's favourite descriptive words is 'outrageous'. What's yours?

2) Which of the following is NOT the kind of thing the Regiment expects to see in a best-selling SAS book:

a) 'I looked up and saw the goatherd at the top of the *wadi*. For a moment time stood still. He was only a young kid but his soul was as old and wise as the desert itself. He saw my gun and smiled a friendly open smile. I smiled back. Two cultures, reaching out for each other in the midst of all this nothingness. And then I slotted him.' ☐

b) 'Ligger was in a bad way. He knew it, I knew it, even the vultures knew it. Forty-three days without anything to eat or drink takes a toll on a man. I decided to go easy on him. "Get the fuck up, you lazy fat Geordie poof," I said. "And if you won't, I will." Ligger staggered to his feet. "Thanks mate," he said. "Let's go and blow up the refinery."' ☐

c) 'Colin had that far-away look in his eyes that meant one thing and one thing only. "Kiss me," I said. "And this time do it like you mean it."' ☐

# MOUSSE'S SELECTION DIARY

**21** Wednesday  DAY ONE - Arrived at Hereford at 10.17 am, two hours late thanks to hippies on the line at Clipping Norton. No dramas. We weren't officially due at Stirling Lines (S.A.S. HQ) till 12.00 am though I still had to find them first - easier said than done when they don't give you directions. I tried to ask a few locals but they all shook their heads and muttered something about 'initiative' and having to get back in time to watch Ready, Steady Cook on the tele.

Decided to wait at the station, spot any likely-looking SAS men and follow them. Eventually two came along - big, strong muscley men in white vests and monstaches. They couldn't've looked more like Regiment if they were wearing Black Kit and dangling from a rope in front of the Iranian Embassy. Fell in behind them as they zig-zagged through the town's busy streets, slowed down and made a sharp right into a large, nondescript building. On the doorway was a small sign: 'Mr Muscle's Gym

**22** Thursday and Sauna'. Inside were lots of naked men sitting on towels. They all also had monstaches and seemed very pleased to see me, especially when I stripped off and revealed my selection of body conditioning lotions and personal hygiene products. Left an hour and a half later none the wiser about where I was going but with sharpened skin tone and, I like to think, just a hint of a tan.

DAY TWO - First day of real training - 30K circular route through the Black Mountains in full kit. Weather terrible, terrain rough & inhospitable. Felt cold, wet and miserable throughout with every bone & muscle in my body stretched to breaking point. Of course it would've been much worse if we'dve had to get out of the lorry.

＊ Six blokes binned for winging and eating their sandwiches before we'd left the squadron car park.

**28** Wednesday

DAY SIX— Another hard, tiring day. Three mile bicycle ride, followed by field watercolour class and a tricky five course lunch involving a wide range of cutlery and a number of testing grand cru wines. Sat next to a bloke called Andy who spent the whole meal listening to everyone else and writing down every word they said in a big red notebook.

✱ Another three blokes binned for poor small-talk and using their soup spoon to dish out the vegetables.

DAY SEVEN— After a week of intensive training that's seen the original 120 brutally whittled down to 111, US survivors are ready for our first big test— the Fan Dance. Pass this and we might, just might, be on our way to being selected. Fail it and well, I might as well have just stayed for the full body massage in the Mr. Muscle Sauna.

Before we set out for the hills made sure I had a nice long bath and sorted my hair out. On Selection blokes use all sorts of weird & wonderful grooming concoctions to give them that vital edge. Some work, others don't. Me, I was taking no chances. I reached into my wash bag & pulled out my biggest gun - Trevor

**29** Thursday     Dolby Systeme seaweed and feta firm hold Shampoo and Conditioning Mousse. If I was gonna go down on the Fan Dance I was gonna go down fighting.

All too soon we were up on Pen-y-Fan in a high wind, pulling on our bergen's and steeling ourselves for the toughest challenge of our lives. In fact I was concentrating so hard that I didn't even hear the music start up and I lost vital seconds before I got out there & went into a nicely controlled pasa double with a staff sergeant Jock 'Cream Puff' McKnee. The wind was gusting like a good 'un and as he spun me into another fast kick turn, I was sure I was going to blow it. And then magically the music stopped. The wind died down. I nervously got out my mirror and checked my hair. Perfect. Not a follicle was out of place. Trevor had come through for me. I looked up at the training officer. He smiled & gave me a little wink. I had done it. From this moment on it was, quite literally, downhill all the way.

✱ 109 blokes binned for not smiling enough, poor comb selection and saying bitchy things about their dancing partners.

DAY EIGHT— Came down to breakfast to find that all of the training staff had got up at dawn & left on the first available Sunshine Coach. Apparently most of them were crying as they got on the bus. It must be hell for them, knowing they can't be here to see us finish the course.

# SIDE SALAD SAYS, 'KNOW YOUR GREENS'

*When you're on a mission, food is one of the most important things in your survival armoury, along with water and knowing exactly when to lift your skirt and make a run for it. Sometimes, of course, you can bring everything you need with you, neatly wrapped in tin foil and tucked out of harm's way near the top of your Bergen. Other times, though, this will be difficult, if not impossible, and you will have to make the most of the banquet that nature has left out for you in situ.*

Nowadays, of course, what with supermarkets and 24-hour home pizza, most of our basic animal foraging skills have been forgotten in a frenzy of packaging and sell-by dates. In the Regiment we have no such luxury. We eat where we sleep where we tab. The Golden Rule is always make the best of what's there. And if there's nothing there you make the best of that too.

## MUSHROOMS

Yum. Whenever I'm in the field on Hard Routine I keep a special look out for Cèpe and Chanterelle. Sometimes these can be found in woodland and shaded areas near fast-flowing rivers. More often than not they're found in Selfridges Food Hall, right next to the Tuscan Purple Rocket rack. At £19.50 a kilo nobody can call them cheap, but they're absolutely delicious on toast with a dab of Worcester sauce and a sprinkle of fresh-ground paprika.

## TOADSTOOLS

I dunno. There are so many different types and the line between the ones you can eat and ones that'll kill you is so thin that I only ever use them on Fijians or visiting journalists.

## GRASS

Useless except for lying in and/or stuffing down the back of Scud's shirt when you

---

### DANGER SIGNS

When you're in the field the first basic assumption you must make is that EVERYTHING that grows, moves or growls is edible – unless of course it's not. How do you know what is and what isn't? Well, there are a few classic danger signs to look out for:

- Sour or rotten taste
- Stinging sensation on the tongue
- Gut-ache
- Burning sensations in the lower bowel
- Vomiting/diarrhoea
- Hallucinations
- Intense muscle-spasms
- Coma
- Death

If you or anyone else on your patrol starts to suffer from any of these, it's probably best to avoid that particular species or plant in future.

really want to annoy him. Apparently there are some strains of South American pampas you can do something with, but you have to wear a cowboy hat and use the word *gringo* without irony first, so I wouldn't bother if I were you.

## NETTLES

Now we're talking. Nettles can be boiled, stir-fried, fricasseed or fermented to produce a passable white wine that goes well with fish and soft cheeses. The hard part is picking the stuff without getting stung to buggery. I recommend using either thick gloves or the services of a nearby Fijian.

## GREEN FOLIAGE

Are you kidding? What am I, an ungulate? You can boil it for days in the finest oyster sauce in Chinatown and it still tastes like something the cat sicked up. Forget it.

## NUTS

Of course you can live on nuts but I tend to use them mainly as field decorations for cakes, sponges and all manner of open and closed tantin tarts. You'd be surprised what a difference they make to a dish. There's nothing that gives me greater pleasure after a hard day of close-quarter enemy contact than to rustle up a nice rum and almond syllabus for the boys' supper. You should see their little faces light up like a petrol tanker on the road to Basra!

## SEAWEED

Yeah. Now don't get me wrong. I know you can eat seaweed. In fact I have done so myself on a number of occasions in all parts of the world. It's one thing though to get it down your neck when you really have to, (i.e. before the crispy Peking duck with pancakes arrives), and quite another to attempt yourself on some God-forsaken sea shore without a decent pair of chopsticks in sight. In X Squadron we mainly use it as a beauty aid, though Scud once put so much into his night-time face pack that his skin turned green. Well, at least it made a change from purple.

## FRUIT & BERRIES

The existence of so many species of fruit and berries on the planet is proof, if proof were needed, that Mother Nature likes a nice pud as much as the next man. Strawberries, raspberries, loganberries, blackberries, wild cherries, apples, pears, papaws – the list is as long as the Amazon, though of course not quite as windy and prone to flash-floods.

With so much abundance you can generally afford to be choosy, so, unless you're really up shit creek, don't put up with anything that the Roux brothers wouldn't be proud to turn into a clarified jelly and spoon over a griddled hare.

**A spot of R & R at the Squadron's annual Barbecue and Buffet – Oman**

# Andy McGrabb's SAS stories
# IRANIAN EMBASSY SIEGE

*I think we all remember what we were doing when our beepers went off. Mousse was plucking his eyebrows, Scud was polishing his wart, Rupert was reading 'Biggles Pulls It Off' and Side Salad had just peeled his crêpes off the griddle. Me and Fiji Bob were arm wrestling. Despite his weight advantage I was doing well. My key tool to success was the surprise element. He wasn't expecting a Heckler & Koch sub-machine pistol with grenade launcher. When we got the call, we snapped instantly into action like a well-oiled war correspondent. I got everyone up to RAE Corps barracks in Beaconsfield for the BWTTYWH (Bit Where They Tell You What's Happening) and learnt the full extent of the covert op. Six men had taken over the Iranian Embassy and were holding hostages. Red Team were going in the front. We were going in the back.*

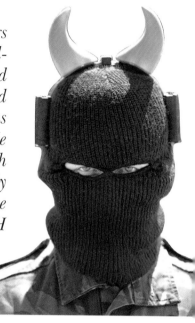

**'War is Hell'**

There was no time for faffing about. The key issue was to get up there as soon as possible, wait for the signal and storm the building. We piled into the Metro and whizzed up the motorway to Kensington with me navigating and Mousse in charge of the radio. He chose Spandau Ballet's 'True' and Ultravox's 'Vienna'. I'd have preferred Madness but you can't undermine your men when you've put them i/c stereo.

In no time I'd located the Embassy building and established a POV from the roof of the fire station behind it. The other lads seemed to be doing well. There was no sign of Red Team although we could hear them on the radio. It's moments like that when you realise what expert camouflage training can do for you. All around us were the men of 22 SAS and yet to a passer by it simply looked like a quiet Kensington street.

**'Officer class – so low on the evolutionary ladder that molluscs ask him for a leg up.'**

The only embuggerance was the shameful behaviour of Fiji Bob. I don't like to peach on a colleague, but the fact is, he panicked and lost heart. One minute he was loading his weapon and scanning the target, the next he was looking over my shoulder at the map and honking that we were in the wrong place.

Your Fijian is a good fighter, but in a tight spot he's prone to flannel and downright cheek. That kind of thing undermines the troop and puts a strain on all of us. The rest of the lads were flapping and it was only a matter of time before Fiji Bob's nonsense started to work on their confidence.

I decided there was only one option. I pointed down into the street and said, 'Look, there's Ratu Ganilau, former president of Fiji.' Bob frowned as he looked down and away from me. 'I thought he was dead,' he muttered as I swung the butt of my M16 against the back of his head. He fell like a dynamited Redwood and we rolled him across the flat roof and into the rain gutter. There's no room for doubts on a covert op. That way lies madness.

A voice crackled over the radio. 'Right. Stand by, stand by. X Squadron, where the fuck are you?' It was clear that the Ruperts were beginning to lose their nerve as well but I replied crisply, 'All in position and ready, Skip.'

I could hear Willie Whitelaw slurping port in the background as they gave the order to attack. Later I heard Maggie Thatcher was chewing the carpet and waving a whisky bottle over her head singing 'Ere we go, 'ere we go.' She's a good sport is Mags. Once, during a training exercise in the Killing House at Hereford, we accidentally set light to her husband and she was really good about it and asked us if we could do Mark next.

We swung over the gap and in through the French windows of the building opposite, throwing grenades ahead of us. We stepped through the rubble and smoke into the room and went into our

The surreptitious infil using a VW Beetle was admired throughout the Services.

rehearsed routine. Mousse and Scud peeled off right and I went left with Side Salad and Rupert. We could hear shooting behind us. It was Scud and Mousse smoking the first of the Marlboros.

We called the enemy 'Marlboros' and the hostages 'Rothmans'. So your target becomes a Marlboro, not a person. Your job is to stub out the Marlboro. Sadly, that day, we got through a pack of twenty Rothmans.

Looking back, we probably should have been suspicious when several of the terrorists appeared to be carrying clipboards. Not your obvious piece of kit for a deranged raghead. Also, one of the ones I shot seemed to be sitting at a computer terminal doing a spread sheet. Again, not your obvious activity for a terrorist, but I knew they'd demanded a ransom and thought she might have been calculating the interest on a PEP.

It was all over in ten minutes. We'd met minimal resistance and those we confirmed as hostages were all lying face down on the lawn. One of the baddies tried to slip away and we pulled him back inside to finish him off.

As he was being dragged back in, one of the woman hostages put her arms tight around his legs and begged us, 'No, no, no, please don't. He's the Deputy Borough Treasurer.' I guess she had formed some sort of bond with her captive. We let him off with a leg wound and chained his neck to a drainpipe.

We were still on a high as we searched the debris for mementoes. Scud decided to half-inch some of the Embassy's notepaper, which was when we found out. His

**War is hell.**

**Fiji Bob recovering from his sighting of ex-president Ratu Ganilau.**

lips moved as he read the legend across the top with slow deliberation: 'London Borough of Kensington Planning Department.'

The truth is, we were let down by our chain of command. It was everyone's job to double-check each other's decisions and calculations. Fiji Bob's failure to make his views known about the navigational discrepancy led to a tragedy for the Regiment and a bit of an embuggerance for the families of the civil servants. There can be no excuse for that. The troop commander has to carry the can, even if one of his men is really responsible for the mishap. That's the heavy burden of command. Which is why I was the first to point out that Rupert outranked me and was therefore technically in charge.

The truth was, Rupert had always been a potential liability. His background frankly made him unsuitable to command a squadron like ours, which was why I took over decision-making on occasion. I spoke up for him at his court martial though. That's the one good thing about the Regiment. When the chips are down, whatever you may think personally, you stand up for your mates. I know they'd all do the same for me. Except Fiji Bob of course, smug bastard.

# WHAT'S IN MY BERGEN?

## Rupert D'eath Cutie

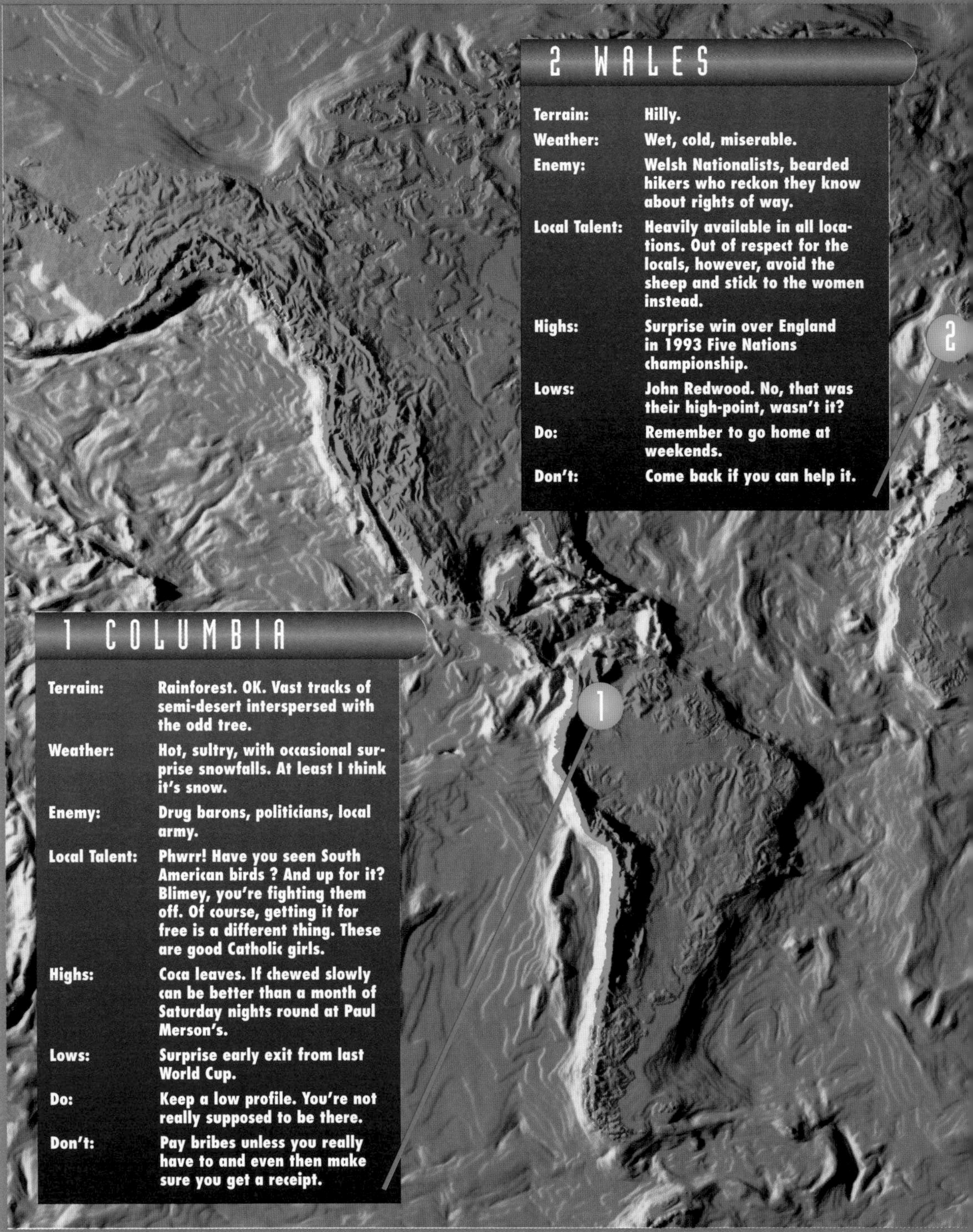

## 2 WALES

| | |
|---|---|
| **Terrain:** | Hilly. |
| **Weather:** | Wet, cold, miserable. |
| **Enemy:** | Welsh Nationalists, bearded hikers who reckon they know about rights of way. |
| **Local Talent:** | Heavily available in all locations. Out of respect for the locals, however, avoid the sheep and stick to the women instead. |
| **Highs:** | Surprise win over England in 1993 Five Nations championship. |
| **Lows:** | John Redwood. No, that was their high-point, wasn't it? |
| **Do:** | Remember to go home at weekends. |
| **Don't:** | Come back if you can help it. |

2

## 1 COLUMBIA

| | |
|---|---|
| **Terrain:** | Rainforest. OK. Vast tracks of semi-desert interspersed with the odd tree. |
| **Weather:** | Hot, sultry, with occasional surprise snowfalls. At least I think it's snow. |
| **Enemy:** | Drug barons, politicians, local army. |
| **Local Talent:** | Phwrr! Have you seen South American birds ? And up for it? Blimey, you're fighting them off. Of course, getting it for free is a different thing. These are good Catholic girls. |
| **Highs:** | Coca leaves. If chewed slowly can be better than a month of Saturday nights round at Paul Merson's. |
| **Lows:** | Surprise early exit from last World Cup. |
| **Do:** | Keep a low profile. You're not really supposed to be there. |
| **Don't:** | Pay bribes unless you really have to and even then make sure you get a receipt. |

1

## 3 LAPLAND

| | |
|---|---|
| Terrain: | Flat subarctic tundra. |
| Weather: | Brass monkeys, mate. |
| Enemy: | Frostbite, wild moose, Christmas shoppers looking for Santa's Grotto. |
| Local Talent: | Drinking. Suicide. Or is that Finland? |
| Highs: | About 3°C above. |
| Lows: | 50°C below. |
| Do: | Shut the door behind you when you come in. There's a terrible draught. |
| Don't: | Just talk about the weather. There are loads of interesting things to say like... like... oh, fuck it. It's a freezer today, isn't it? |

## 5 BRUNEI

| | |
|---|---|
| Terrain: | Jungle. |
| Weather: | Hot & steamy with bursts of tropical rainfall whenever you try to play cricket. |
| Enemy: | Mossies, scorpions, vampire bats, dysentery, foot-rot, flash-floods... do you really want me to go on? |
| Local Talent: | Tricky. Any half decent-looking bird is instantly whisked away towards the Sultan's palace before you can say 'training bra'. You could try your luck with the pygmies, but you'll have to build them a hut and wrestle a python before they'll go beyond heavy petting. |
| Highs: | Waking up in the morning alive. |
| Lows: | Waking up in the morning dead. |
| Do: | Bring a spare pair of socks. |
| Don't: | Wear them - they'll only get dirty. |

## 4 OMAN

| | |
|---|---|
| Terrain: | Sand. |
| Weather: | Hot. |
| Enemy: | Boredom, sand, heat. |
| Local Talent: | Sparse, though locals have been known to try to sell you their daughters for a can of Red Stripe and a Simpson's T-Shirt. After a month in the desert even the female camels can look worryingly attractive. |
| Highs: | Flight home. |
| Lows: | Flight in. |
| Do: | Bring a bucket, a spade and a nice paperback. |
| Don't: | Make it a Jeffrey Archer. Even the Sudan isn't that boring. |

3

4

5

# Andy McGrabb's Guide to Fitness

**You've got to be fit in the Regiment. Very fit. That goes without saying. But you've also got to be sensible. Look at your average Olympic athlete. He trains every day for hours at a stretch, in fact he does nothing but train. Then what happens – he gets laid up with a dodgy hamstring, a ropey groin or your common head cold. You can be too fit. So don't overdo it. Here's a little exercise you can do to ensure you stay in trim without risking serious injury.**

## The Remote Control

Throw it away! Sounds radical, but you'd be amazed how this simple gesture can improve the quality of your life. Obviously, the first few days will hurt like hell. You'll sit on the sofa watching the telly with your index finger itching worse than a mozzy bite that's gone septic. But with time and will power you can conquer it. Certainly it will be tough the first few times you go out in public. You'll find yourself drifting into your local Radio Rentals and copping a quick feel of a remote when the assistant isn't looking. But, with time, this too will pass.

And, on the plus side, you'll find yourself walking an extra mile a day. Further, if you're really tough on yourself, push your sofa back another few feet from the telly.

COMBAT

# METHODS OF CONCEALMENT

*W*hen the Gulf War kicked off, we were all bursting to get out there. Me, because I wanted to do my bit, Mousse because his tan had started to fade, Side Salad because he wanted to try his hand at cous cous and 'Scud' (then known as 'Oi you') because he hadn't yet decided on a nickname. We were all honking when the Bravo missions were handed out and those tossers from A Squadron were selected. We had far more writing experience than them. But our time soon came and it wasn't long before we were crouched in the back of a 109 waiting to be set down in the desert sands of Iraq.

I'd put Side Salad i/c kit packing which must have been really thorough as the Bergens weighed twice as much as Fiji Bob by the time we got them on. Despite the weight, I was a bit mystified when Side Salad told me we wouldn't be using hexy blocks to brew up. 'What the fuck are we using then?' I asked. He pointed to a large square crate at one end of the chopper as the loadies pushed it out over the drop zone. 'Traditional Farmhouse Aga,' he said. 'Very good for baking. Needs blacking once a week of course, and we probably shouldn't use the grill at night in case the ragheads spot the flames.'

I was flapping as we made the jump. This was a real embuggerance. Why had I let the stupid Taff pack the kit? We'd never find enough wood in the desert for the Aga and besides, they're all right for casseroles, but rubbish for toast. As it turned out the Aga had a real result. Its canopy failed to open and it landed on an Iraqi tank. When we got back I recommended it for a DSM. It was only right.

Like all the Bravo missions, we suffered from faulty intelligence. The spooks swore blind the area would be really hot and we felt really bone standing in the freezing cold wearing Hawaiian shirts and bermudas. Only Mousse looked good. He had a Sta-Prest button-down shirt and denim culottes under his kit. I was impressed. I had no idea 'Next' did webbing.

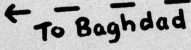

Fiji Bob's route

← To Baghdad

The first thing was to establish a CP (Cowering Point), scout the area and get a bead on the Scud sites. Fiji Bob had the body weight for a long tab and ate a lot of carrots so I sent him out to Close Target Recce the surrounding terrain under cover of darkness. Whilst he was gone, I got on the TACBE and tried to give the OC a sitrep. Orders came back to find and destroy the nearest Scud site, strangle a few goatherds and exfil via the 109 at the EVAC RV.

Neutralising the goatherds was important. Most of the Bravo missions did severe damage to the Iraqis' goat herding capability, and animals were still wandering free across the desert three months after the conflict doing untold damage.

I asked Side Salad to get a fix on our position using the Magellan Satellite Navigation Tool, but apparently it was a choice between packing that and the microwave, so we fell back on our training and looked for trees with moss on one side. Sadly, intelligence failed us once again as they had neglected to inform us that foliage was at a premium in the desert.

As it happened, we had other things to think about as shots rang out from above the *wadi*. Scud had been on stag and by the time we got our arses up to his LUP it was all over. He'd spotted three targets making good progress up to our position and had quickly taken them out before we were compromised. Vultures are tricky customers and can reveal your position by hovering overhead, so Scud had made a good decision. But one had got away and was already winging its way back across the plain.

Things were beginning to go badly wrong and, as patrol commander, I held myself to blame. When the chips are down, you have to take responsibility, so I opted to stay put and call in the chopper for immediate exfil. No sense going on with a compromised team. That would have been outrageous. Whilst we waited for the chopper, I got a brew on. It was a long wait and, as dawn broke, the lads were shivering badly. I decided the only way to avoid exposure was to get them up and moving around.

Rupert was just coming out to bat, needing a half century to avoid the follow-on, when we had

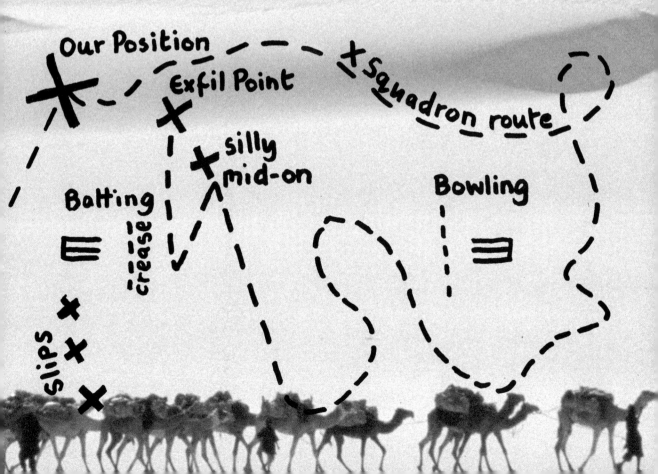

the contact. We found out later that the Iraqis had got a fix on our position from Mousse's mobile phone. Apparently they'd traced a call to his broker and moved a Scud launcher out to a firing position. This was when poor old Scud got his nickname. He had just been bowled out and was walking in to garrotte the umpire (Achmed the goatherd) when the missile landed. If it hadn't been for his cricket box and pads he would have been a dead man.

When the chopper finally arrived, Bravo Nine Nine Nine had taken quite a few casualties. I'd broken a tooth on one of Side Salad's Ciabatta rolls, Rupert strained his groin whilst bowling, Scud had whiplash from nutting shrapnel, Mousse had sunburn and desperately needed to moisturise and Side Salad got olive oil down his shorts. Oh, and Fiji Bob lost two fingers blowing up a Scud launcher but totally failed to RV with the chopper and had to tab 400 miles across enemy territory. There's no excuse for that sort of thing.

**Achmed's controversial lbw judgement.**

MCGRABB: Bravo 999 to Big Welly. SITREP follows. APC located with PNG at 1200. GPS is U/S. CO negative RTU with ERV. Will FRV at FOB with COP whilst CTR MSR's. Do you read, over?.

HQ: Come again, Bravo?

MCGRABB: E& E compromised. DF U/S. TACBE lost in cuds. DPM's not matching SHREDDIES. CO LBW. We're bulking up here. Tell AWACS to ID TEL themselves and exfil by 109. Over.

HQ: No. Still not getting it. Who's Tel?

MCGRABB: Look just come and get us in one of those whirly things and bring five pairs of clean trousers.

**Transcript of radio messages sent from X Squadron to Combined Forces HQ in Riyadh from behind Iraqi lines – July 12th 3.30pm**

# THE SAS GUIDE TO
# CHRISTMAS

Domestically speaking, Christmas is the big one. It's the Gulf War, the Falklands Conflict and Vietnam all rolled into one. And it comes once a year. To survive you have to plan meticulously, prepare yourself against any eventuality and know your enemy. In my personal case, Great Uncle Fred, who technically isn't even a relation but turns up every year regardless and attempts to disrupt proceedings.

## MIDNIGHT MASS

The first big set piece of the whole shebang. The vital thing is to establish a decent LUP. One which is prominent enough so that members of the community can see that you are a regular churchgoer but not so prominent that they can see you taking some precautionary shut-eye while the Vicar's gobbing off.

To achieve this I get the family to cover every entrance. Kimberley tabs up the aisle, the twins take a portal apiece and I'm i/c the nave. Our aim is to RV at the ninth aisle back on the left hand side of the church. This is my preferred LUP in our local church because:

• There is a sturdy pillar which provides cover and

IDEAL LUP

much-needed shelter.

• It is a handy OP from which you can see the Head Shed reading the lesson. But he can't see you.

• You are within tabbing distance of the MSR which runs up through the centre of the church to the altar. Very useful for collecting provisions (dried bread and wine) half-way through the service.

## GOD

You can't ignore Uncle God at Christmas. He is the big player. The Supreme Being. Without him the show might never have gone up. A sobering thought.

Over the Christmas period I try to spare a few moments for Uncle God. We go back a long way.

UNCLE GOD FAILS TO DO THE BUSINESS

During training, when I was marooned from the rest of my men and nursing a watery coffee in a service station outside Fishguard, the Supreme Being appeared just over the right-hand corner of the fruit machine. In a trance, I disengaged the required bit of shrapnel from my pocket, slotted it into the machine and pulled the lever. Whirrr, whirr, whirr. 'If you help me now, I'll be your best fucking mate forever,' I pleaded. 'If you're there, do it, and I'll be putting pennies in your pot forever'.

It came up lemon, orange, plum. There wasn't even a nudge. God did not exist.

## CHRISTMAS DINNER

The second big contact of the proceedings. Usually develops into one helluva fire-fight. The important man to watch like a hawk is Great Uncle Fred. He's as dangerous as jundie with an inflamed chutney ferret, and he knows it. To counter this I like to take up position at the head of the table which gives me a good OP on the action. At the other end I place Kimberley, and down one side attempt to neutralise Great Uncle Fred by putting him between the twins.

For their own protection no one sits in front of GUF. Christmas '93, he bulked up horribly all over the new pastel sweater with regimental logo Kimberley had just given me. I thought I was going to die.

Since that moment I keep eye-to-eye on GUF at all times. The eyes give so much away. They are a window into what's left of GUF's mind. They tell you when he's happy, when he's sad, when he's alert, when he's bluffing and, most importantly, when he's going to bulk all over your sweater.

## THE QUEEN'S SPEECH AND GIFTS

For me, and I suspect the rest of the nation, Her Majesty taking the time to talk to her subjects makes everything worthwhile. In as little as fifteen minutes this wonderful woman can put the 'Great' back into Britain. Long live our noble Queen. As a family we watch the whole speech standing to attention and I don't give the command 'Easy' until the theme music for the Christmas edition of *Top of the Pops* is well under way.

Since Kimberley gave me a video recorder, birthday '88, and immeasurably improved my life, I have taped every one of HM's speeches. In moments of stress some people turn to drugs, some to Paul McKenna. I turn to this tape.

After HM everything is liable to be a disappointment. Like everyone else we try to mask this disappointment by the meaningless gesture of giving each other presents at 1600 hours. It doesn't work.

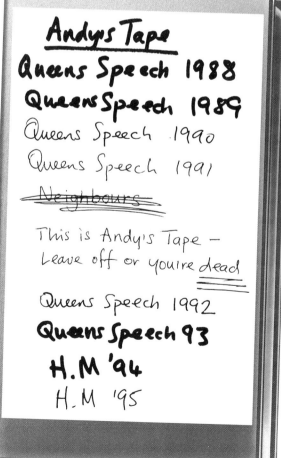

NEW AGE
THERAPY

AGAS OVER IRAQ
HARRY PRYCE DCM MM
SOON TO BE THE STAR OF A MAJOR SIX-PART BBC SERIES 'OUT OF THE FRYING PAN, INTO THE FIRE', HARRY PRYCE DCM MM HAS BROUGHT OUT A VIDEO THAT WILL NESTLE SNUGLY INTO YOUR CHRISTMAS STOCKING.
INCLUDES
MAKE THE MOST OF YOUR HEXY
CORDON BLEU COOKING WITH A CAN OF BEANS
LET'S HEAR IT FOR WORLD CUISINE
AS SEEN ON READY STEADY COOK
£12.99

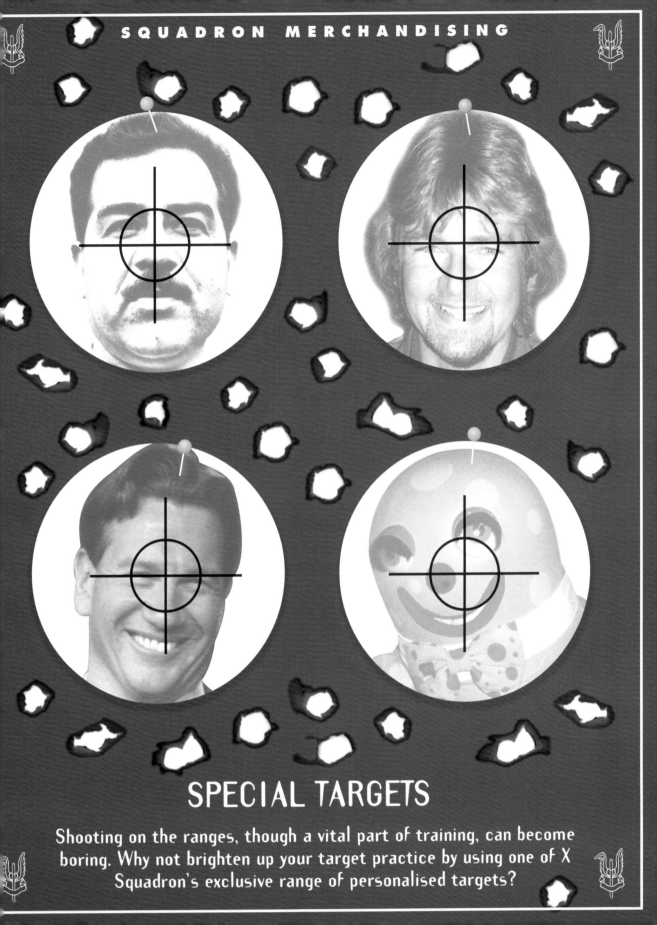

# SPECIAL TARGETS

Shooting on the ranges, though a vital part of training, can become boring. Why not brighten up your target practice by using one of X Squadron's exclusive range of personalised targets?

# SCUD'S GUIDE TO WINNIN

Let's be having you, if the Regiment were invited to take part in the Royal Tournament, we'd piss it. Year after year nancies from Davenport, Portsmouth and The Fleet Air Arm turn up and embarrass the hell out of the harder element in the Armed Forces.

As a recruiting exercise it's a shambles; as a sporting event it's a nonsense. The following radical changes must be made immediately.

### FORGET AUNTIE, SELL THE RIGHTS TO SKY

Say what you like about Mr Murdoch, his boys know how to cover a sporting event. And, perhaps more importantly, are prepared to shell out big moolah for the privilege.

First thing to do, then, is to get on the dog and bone to Rupe and sell him the exclusive rights to the Royal Tournament until the millennium after the next one. Second thing to do is put the big cheque in a high-interest deposit account.

### THE TOURNAMENT MUST BECOME INTERNATIONAL

There's no room for sentiment or loyalty in this game, so it's P45 time for the boys from Davenport, Portsmouth and The Fleet Air

**Let's keep the horses out of it. The last battle they played a major role in was the Charge of the Light Brigade and that wasn't exactly a result.**

Arm. They're out on their ears, and we're on the air. My ideal line-up would see the Regiment competing against a team from the Foreign Legion, a side made up of ex-members of the Stasi and a Pan European Invitation Terrorists XI. That would get the punters flocking back to Earls Court.

### FOR GOD'S SAKE, GET SOME DECENT ANALYSTS IN

Fans of Monday Night Football need no reminding that Andy Gray is the pundit's pundit. No one is as comfortable on the chalkboard as him or can work a video machine so effortlessly. He's a must sign, around whom I intend to build my dream panel. Linking up with Andy, I would like to see General Sir John Hackett given the chance to see what he can do. The General may be a bit long in the tooth but his experience could prove invaluable. Next, a bit of glamour. Now, quite a few people

# HE ROYAL TOURNAMENT

**Notice the Vauxhall sign – they sponsor non-league football. Says it all really.**

knocked Anthea Turner for her work on the Lottery but, personally, I think she's under-rated and could develop a nice line in studio banter with the General. Finally, an irritating git whom the public love to hate. Step forward, Anne Diamond.

So, there you have it, Scud's Dream Panel: Gray, Hackett, Turner and Diamond.

## MAKE IT SEXY

At present, the whole Tournament suffers from a lack of realism. I mean, how often, out there in the real world, are you going to have to assemble a field gun and then take it up and down a stadium? Not often.

To give the event a bit of much-needed zing, I'd lose the Field Gun and replace it with a re-enactment of a contact using live ammunition. That would sort out the sheep from the goats.

To give the event an even more needed touch of sophistication, I would have bikinied dolly birds high-legging it around the stadium in between each round. Like they do in the boxing.

## CONCLUSION

Following the above would make the Royal Tournament the highest-rating show in television history, instead of a pile of shite. Thank you, Scud.

# Finances

*When it comes to adding up anything other than the number of jundies slotted of a summer's afternoon, your average member of the Regiment struggles. However, we are all responsible adults and fully capable of dealing with adult responsibilities.*

## Mortgages

If you're going to die tomorrow, there's no point wasting time dicking around organising yourself a mortgage. Let's face it, by the time all the repayments are made, you'll have been propping up daisies for a couple of decades. All the top people in the Regiment rent. You can get in and out quickly and, if tidy, leave no trace that you've ever been there.

## Pensions

If you're going to die tomorrow, there's no point wasting time dicking around organising yourself a pension. Let's face it, by the time you're eligible to pick up your free bus pass and twenty-odd quid a week you'll have been propping up daisies for three or four decades. At least. As far as the Regiment are concerned, if they discover you've taken out a pension they reckon you've lost your bottle and you're RTU'd a.s.a.p.

## Life Insurance

If you're going to die tomorrow, there's absolutely every point spending your last twenty-four hours on the planet getting as much life insurance as you can lay your hands on. The trouble is that the civvies who work in life insurance aren't as stupid as they sound. No high street firm, not even Churchill, will offer life insurance to a bloke who has crashed through their front window with his Heckler and Koch blazing.

There is, however, one patriotic firm who offer terms to members of the Regiment. Not, it has to be said, the most generous of terms, as the following table illustrates.

| Cause of Death | Premium | Pay-out |
|---|---|---|
| **Friendly Fire:** | £1,000 per annum | £1,000 |
| **Death during Training:** | £1,000 per annum | £2,000 |
| **Death from Insect Bites:** | £1,000 per annum | £5,000 |
| **Death from Exposure:** | £1,000 per annum | £5,000 |
| **Death from Food Poisoning:** | £1,000 per annum | £5,000 |
| **Death in Battle: (caused by own incompetence)** | £1,000 per annum | £5,000 |
| **Death in Battle: (caused by enemy fire)** | £1,000 per annum | £10,000,000 |

# SQUADRON MERCHANDISING

# SUPPORT YOUR BOYS

by purchasng one of this range of Regimental products, all carrying the Regimental logo and exclusively available to readers of this book.

All white, some cotton T-shirts.
Make your choice from the following:

YOU'VE BEEN SLOTTED

THATCHER SLOTTED

only £19.99

MY DAD WENT TO THE GULF WAR AND ALL I GOT WAS THIS LOUSY T-SHIRT

SHOOT FIRST. IF ANYONE ASKS ANY QUESTIONS, SHOOT THEM AS WELL

Make all cheques payable to A. McGrabb Esq and send to P.O. Box Bravo Two Zero, Isle of Man.

Allow as long as it takes for delivery.

## Operation Motherload I

FRANKFURT. A single word chalked onto the briefing board in Sec Ops, like a lonely sentry with no one else around him in the middle of an otherwise empty desert. For a long time we all sat in silence staring up at it, letting the vast implications of these nine little letters sink in. Eventually a couple of the lads made their move. They reached down to their boots, got out their pencils, wrote it down and started to memorise it. The rest just sat perfectly still, taking it all in, missing nothing. This, we knew instantly with almost a sixth sense, was going to be one of those once-in-a-lifetime missions that you lie awake at night praying will come your way. Sometimes you get lucky. Sometimes you don't. This time we'd all rolled a double six and landed on Mayfair before anyone had built any hotels on it. Scud looked particularly thoughtful as he leant back in his chair and rolled himself another of his disgusting cigarettes. 'Frankfurt,' he said in his thick Geordie accent. 'As in, like, you know, Germany? It was. Rupert nodded gravely. 'Yup. Now why don't one of you chaps make us a brew and we'll start on a plan.'

A tremor of excitement went around the room. Although we'd had our fair share of action in the last couple of months, it had been mainly routine, run-of-the-mill work guarding visiting heads of state and acting as extras in another SAS series. Now it was the real thing, and we all knew that it would demand every ounce of skill and stamina that all those long years of training had prepared us for.

The men would be looking to me, as platoon leader, for clear, decisive decision-making and leadership. As far as I was concerned they could have it with bells on. 'OK,' I said clearly and decisively. 'Mousse – get the kettle on. Side Salad – you're i/c biscuits. Fiji Bob – cover us.' The men leapt up to perform their various tasks like cogs in a well-oiled machine. Literally within minutes we were sitting in close briefing-circle formation, with steaming mugs of lapsang souchong and a plate of authentic Viennese whirls that Side Salad had lifted from Harrods during an otherwise uneventful RPJ (Royal Protection Job). The tea was fresh, sweet and hit the back of your throat like a sucker-punch in a playground brawl. The Viennese whirls were quality kit as well – though Side Salad did get a bit upset when Scud dunked his in for just that one killer second too long, and lost the whole lot down the front of his trousers.

At last we were ready for the most important thing any group of SAS can ever do together (apart of course from blasting the shit out of a lorry-load of rag-heads) – planning. What we said now, in the next few precious minutes, would determine everything about the success or failure of the task in hand. Everyone had their part to play and it was Golden Rule that no man's voice went unheard, unless he was either Fiji Bob, who never, ever said anything, or Rupert, who was an officer and therefore only ever spoke total bollocks.

As per standard procedure, we started with questions: how were we going in, how would we get out, what equipment would we need, what equipment would we take even if we didn't need it, where would we be stopping off for a drink on the way back? As usual, the thorny issue of transport proved the most sticky. I took it upon myself to outline the problem.

'Now, Frankfurt, as Scud has correctly pointed out, is in Germany. Germany is on the other side of the Channel. I would say that pretty much rules out going on foot.'

'What about the Tunnel?', said Scud. 'If push came to shove, we could tab through it in a night, no bother.'

'What about the trains?' said Mouse, ever the realist.

'Fuck the trains. We're the SAS, man.'

'I meant, why don't we get on one of them? Eurostar is very reasonable, as long as you book in advance, and there's lots of luggage space, so we can take as much kit as we need.'

'Or we could always fly,' said Rupert quietly. 'Lufthansa are very good.' Suddenly the room froze as fast as a naked pecker on a night-tab on Brynmawr. We looked at Rupert. 'Sorry,' he said. 'Just thinking out loud.'

'Well, think out quiet, you public-school twat,' said Scud jovially. 'Or I'll shoot your posh bollocks off.' Rupert looked at the floor. As usual he had no answer to Scud's devastating wit and spent the rest of the night making more tea and putting whitener on his tennis pumps. I decided it was time to move on to more important matters.

'OK, boys. What's it gonna be? Pizza or Indian?'

# Fiji Bob

# The SAS *Kama Sutra*

## EQUIPMENT

### BASIC KIT FOR SEXUAL ACTIVITY IS

- A tube of K-Y Jelly – for lubrication. Essential for giving your boots a new lease of life. The modern fighting man can't afford to waste time on foreplay, conversation or indeed any form of relationship that cannot be terminated in 30 seconds with air support.
- An excuse – we're only human. For Christ's sake, we've been slotting all day.
- A valid passport – for speedy exfiltration, preferably by chopper.
- The element of surprise – lay down a good arc of bullshit to cover you before advancing. Check for booby traps and ensure that the terrain allows the use of minefields to prevent target's departure before penetration. If resistance is likely, soften up defences with 28 days of carpet bombing.

## POSITIONING:

For security reasons, the bog standard face-to-face missionary position is a no-no. It allows your sexual partner (always a potential foe, particularly after the carpet bombing) to take advantage of your unprotected rear. How many times have you been pounding away only to find a small child support agency query protruding from your back? Of course, there are ways of minimising the risk, such as tying the hands or anaesthetising, which, although pleasurable, may put you at a disadvantage with your partner. It also makes it really hard to get your clothes back on. But basically there is only one safe sexual position for rock hard members of the SAS. The Fido or 'doggy' position.

This stance allows you to prevent your 'doggy' partner (or pedigree chum) from stealing a psychological advantage by looking at your eyes and saying things like 'Perhaps if you thumb it in?' or 'Do you need me here for this?' It is best to adopt this position close to an open doorway to aid speedy withdrawal.

## REMEMBER

Never give her your real name, rank or serial number. Try sticking to your pen name.

### CONTRACEPTION

Any responsible soldier knows the value of a good packet of three. For example, in the absence of brown hessian sacks, condoms make great substitute sandbags and may also be adapted for use as pressure sensitive land mines. Of course condoms also have a role to play in sexual encounters and if you find you've run out, empty a sandbag and use a brown hessian sack instead. It's a bit scratchy, but a great way of disguising your identity when the balaclava's in the wash.

### AIDS

If you're really short, a chair can be very useful.

# THE FOUR
## *Stages of Seduction*

**1** Select Target

**2** Advance Cautiously

**3** First Contact

**4** Withdrawal

**CRUNCHH!**

| NAME | *The Iraqis* | *The Irish* |
|---|---|---|
| NICKNAME | Rag-heads | Micks; Paddies; Practice |
| LIKELY CONTACT POINT | Iraq; Kuwait; Stringfellows | Ireland; North London buildin sites; Eurovision Song Contes |
| UNIFORM | Desert DPMs; dodgy moustaches; shiny suits | Jeans; beards; jumpers their Granny knitted them for Christmas |
| WEAPONS/ FIGHTING STYLE | AK 47's; Scud Missiles; goats | Armalites; rocket launchers; long, boring monologues abou the potato famine |
| WEAK POINTS | Can be a bit excitable, especially when you've dropped uninvited into their country by helicopter and wasted a couple of hundred of their mates. | Alcohol; Catholic guilt about sex; the Gee-Gees |
| STRONG POINTS | Deeply unpopular, so you can kill and maim thousands of them in your books without losing the sympathies of the reader. | Anecdotes. Most Micks are experts in the black arts of ha to-hand storytelling. NEVER into a close contact exchange narrative fire unless possessec infinite patience, a strong bla der and an infinite number of tales of your own to return fir with. |
| DO SAY | 'No, please, smoke one of mine'; 'Hmm. Nice gold bath taps' | 'My round'; 'Anybody know Delaney's Donkey?' |
| DON'T SAY | 'Shalom'; 'Anyone smell gas?' | 'What do you mean, 1916? Th was ages ago mate' |

If there's one Golden Rule of the SAS – it's know your enemy. Study this top secret wall-chart until your eyeballs bleed.

| he Israelis | Americans | Subversives | The Police |
|---|---|---|---|
| e Israelis | Yanks; Glory Boys | Lefties; Hippies; Ravers; Poofs | Plod; Blue-arsed wankers |
| ...ael; Palestine; wherever they ...el threatened, i.e, everywhere | Any place where there's a short but-decisive victory to be had against opponents infinitely weaker than themselves. | Road protests; marches; Liberal Democrat coffee mornings | High pressure terrorist sieges; pub brawls in Hereford; speeding at 110 mph down the M4 |
| ...isp US-style fatigues; designer ...des; armour-plated bras ...omen soldiers only) | Shorts; annoying baseball caps; Simpsons T-Shirts | Kaftans; goatee beards; Paul Smith sandals | Call that a uniform? |
| ...perts in all aspects of surprise, ...luding abrupt changes to ...ace treaties and devastating ...acks on unarmed refugee ...mps. | Yanks are nothing if not kitted up. In fact they've got so much bloody weaponry they don't know what to do with it, other than crash it into the ground or turn it on their own side. | Unlike the good old days when you could rely on students and the unemployed for a decent tear-up, subversives nowadays tend to take a non-violent, passive stance and make you hit them first. This, of course, is better than nothing, but does rather take some of the fun out of it. | Truncheons; pointless sarcasm; ability to sit around in vans for months on end on overtime |
| ...n be hot-headed, especially ...und election time or when ...yone mentions how much ...ney they get from America. | Yanks like instant success, and so entirely fail to see how we like to fight on the good old-fashioned British basis of coming from behind to snatch an unlikely victory in extra time. They also don't really understand the point of fighting any war or military conflict that can't be made into a Hollywood blockbuster. | Whatever they're protesting about, subversives are generally united by a) their grossly sentimental attitude towards animals and b) a strong fashion sense. Always attack, therefore, on these two fronts by either a) getting weepy about cruelty to goldfish, or b) telling them that you read in *The Face* that tree-hugging went out months ago. | The Police are terrible ditherers and often make a bad situation worse by poncing around with megaphones trying to resolve situations through peaceful negotiation. Worse still for a front-line force, their basic combat/contact skills are lamentable. When was the last time you saw a policeman lay an anti-personnel mine or abseil out of a helicopter? |
| ...ud, decisive people with little ...e for namby-pamby liberal ...eties. Everyone's a fighter in ...ael, which can be a very stir-...g thing – as anyone who's ...er seen a sexy, 20-year-old ...se blasting away with a ...zooka can testify. | TV coverage; press conferences; euphemisms like collateral damage | Subversives are EVERYWHERE and you can easily find yourself out-numbered and running low on ammo if you try to take them all at once. Instead, why not be selective? Only eradicate those that are known to you personally, are the teenage offspring of friends and family or who try to beg money off you when you're coming out of Sainsbury's. | Sealing things off with tape. That's about it, basically. |
| ...n eye for an eye, a tooth for a ...th, a Scud for a Scud' | 'Gee. I don't know where we'd be without you guys' | 'Genesis. Now that's a proper band' | 'Fuck off Filth. We're the SAS' |
| ...y chance of a quick brew up ...d a bacon sarnie?' 'Come on, ...mit it. You have got nuclear ...apons, haven't you?' | 'Vietnam'; 'Cover me'; 'Do you really have to whoop like that every time we slot someone?' | 'Of course I'm not a real security guard you slack-arsed little creep' | 'OK Officer. They're all yours' |

COMBAT

# METHODS OF CONCEALMENT II

RIGHT

WRONG

RIGHT

WRONG

# THAT

REGIMENTAL PIN-UP

# CHER

TERRIFYING GLORY

## Operation Motherload II

FRANKFURT, or, as the Krauts call it, Frankfurt am Main, is a large industrial city that lies on the river Main about 32.73 km east of the Rhine. It has an area of 222 sq km (86 sq miles) and lies in a valley 88 to 212 m (290 to 695 ft) above sea level. Its climate, like the German back four, is cool, calm and collected. The mean temperature is -1°C (30°F) in January and 19°C (66°F) in July. The annual precipitation is about 675 mm (27 in), but fortunately this tends to fall over the year as a whole rather than in one day, so flooding isn't really a major concern. The average tram ride cost 3DM. Dogs are allowed only in the outside areas of licensed cafés.

So much for the dictionary definition. To us Frankfurt meant one thing and one thing only. Trouble. Capital T. Capital Bull. But then again that's exactly how we liked it. No one puts their arse on the line for something beginning with a small letter.

After a whole night of planning with the REMFS, we decided we would go in using IBVR (Infil By Various Routes). This is an old but reliable Regiment tactic that confuses the enemy and lessens the risk of being compromised before you can RV at your LUP and get a brew on. At least, that's the idea. In reality, IBVR's can be a severe embuggerance for everybody, entailing diffuse risk exposure, logistical support difficulties and lots of hanging around at dodgy caffs waiting for stragglers to show up. Still, what with everyone honking everyone else and Rupert still sulking, it seemed the only way to go if we weren't to end up with another messy blue-on-blue. Luckily Head-Shed agreed, and within 24 hours we were packed and ready to go.

To this day I don't know why it took over a week for everyone to reassemble in Frankfurt. Of course some routes took longer than others to execute – nobody could seriously expect Scud to cycle down overnight – but some of the excuses were, frankly, quite outrageous. Side Salad was one of the worst culprits, finally returning rolling from a six-day gourmet tour of the Rhône-Saône valley with a Bergen full of top-quality Riesling and a stupid smile on his face. Mousse was no better, despite the fact that he flew himself straight into RAF Baden-Baden in a drop-wing Cessna. I wasted no time in telling him I couldn't give a monkey's toss whether or not Karl Lagerfeld had invited him over to try out his new power shower. The mission always came first. He should only stop if absolutely necessary to maintain his cover story... which didn't include poncing around with local lingerie salesmen.

Still, at last we were ensconced behind enemy lines, so I ordered the two reprobates out on a CTR while I got on the scaley kit and wired in sit rep to the FOB (Forward Operations Base), which in this case turned out to a bloke with a mobile phone in Marks and Spencers on the main square. His orders were chilling in their simplicity. 'You are compromised. Enemy know you are here but not why. Proceed with caution. Oooh. By the way, they don't take Switch over here.'

I gathered the boys round and filled them in. As I saw it, we had two choices. Either scrap the whole thing now and exfil a.s.a.p. using E&E (Escape and Evasion) where necessary, or stick with it and see what kind of reception the World's Most Boring Army has lined up for us. It really wasn't that hard to decide. As Scud put it, 'We're the fucking Regiment. They're the fucking Krauts. We haven't come all this way to go back again. Besides, I have to stay at least one Saturday or me Eurostar ticket's invalid.' With the decision made we immediately sprang into action and looked around to see how far we were from the target area. We CTR'd, COP'd. We put on our NVG's. We took readings on the Magellan. Nothing. We could have been anywhere. Eventually Fiji Bob strolled back and casually pointed up the street to a large glass building with revolving doors and a large sign marked 'Holiday Inn'. Bingo.

I went stag, with Scud behind me and the rest spread out behind in a special formation called 'Shoppers Wandering Around

With Plastic Bags'. With Scud behind me I knew that if there was a drama he would do the business, drop on one knee, pull out his Minimi and lay down an arc of covering fire. Who knows? With luck and the right wind he might even hit something. We crossed the road and headed towards the revolving doors. There was one elderly German on stag, guarding the doors as though his life depended on it. How right he was. 'It's OK,' I told Scud. 'I'll drop him.' I reached into my inside pocket, unclipped my holster and neutralised the threat in an instant with the business end of a 50 DM note. A moment later we were in, piling into the main reception and establishing ERV's (Emergency Rendezvous) by the Chicago Mudpackers Rib Hut.

Once everyone was in position I got on the headset. 'OK boys,' I whispered. 'This is it. Remember what we're about to do is not just for us but the Squadron as a whole. Fuck this one up and everyone's in the shit.' There were muttered murmurings of assent. 'Let's do it'.

We moved off towards the ballroom. All around us were guys in suits. Some had glasses. The others just looked as though they should. Above the door was a big sign: 'Frankfurt Book Fair'.

I caught Scud's eye and winked. He smiled back. In that instant we both knew that this was one action that would make everything we've ever done seem worthwhile. I reached in the case, took out a thick manuscript and burst through the doors firing out numbers and publication dates. The poor little fuckers never stood a chance.

**THE FIJIAN ZODIAC**

## Fiji Bob's STARS

### Portillop
**AUG 22-SEPT 21**

PORTILLOP is an earth sign. Wet, cloddy and clinging, PORTILLOPS are used as an emetic in some parts of the UK and as a tranquiliser everywhere else. Just listening to a PORTILLOP can be a splendid cure for insomnia. The only time they are even vaguely exciting is when they propose lunatic plans such as selling the Navy for scrap and turning the RAF into a commercial airline.

**THIS WEEK**
Jupiter's familiar aspect in the heavens may signal a return to the pit from whence you came. i.e: Bilbao. Last ditch desperation forces you to once again mention how frightened Europe is of the SAS loudly until everyone wakes up and asks for a benzedrine. Towards the end of the week you will try to keep a straight face when addressing a small crowd with the words 'Ask not what you can do for your country but what you can do for me.'

Lucky sandwich: Speedy Gonzales with chilli sauce.
Lucky After Shave: Tetrion chin filler.

# WILLS AND LAST

Every man who joins the Regiment knows that they're signing up for one of the most dangerous jobs in the world. Death and serious injury stalk your every move like a particularly clingy childhood friend. As professionals we learn to accept this and make sure that all our affairs are tidied up and ready to go at any time.

The way most people do this is in the form of a farewell letter. Of course it isn't always easy to write your last words to your loved ones or financial advisors, so, to help you, we've put together some prime examples of our own fond farewells. Help yourself. Copy word for word if you like, though ideally you should probably change the names to avoid confusion.

Dear Julie — Well darling, looks like I ~~finely~~ finally got the big red card from the great "Ref in the sky. It's a real shame. I still had so much to do. One more weekend and I could have finished off the kitchen. Still, that's the way it goes.

Listen luv I gotta say something. I know we got the two girls and don't get me wrong they're luvely kids. But it would have bin nice to have had a son to carry on the name and all that. Just in case you felt the same way I put a couple of loads of my finest love cream in the # lolley maker in the freezer so you can get it injected into you and make anothes Scud now I'm gone. If you don't want it I'll understand. You can alwayz give it to a sperm bank. Make a change from all those good for nuffin students passing their laziness and commie ideas onto the next ~~generash~~ generation. Gotta go now and save the world from terrorists and foriegn bastards who threaten the British way of life. Tell the girls to be good or they won't get any more clothes for their Barby at Christmas. Remember, I may have gone but you can be shure I took a whole coachload of rag-heads with me

See ya mate

## Scud

P.S Are you sure about those tiles around the sink. If it hadn't bean for them I'm sure I cood've finished the job

# LETTERS HOME...

Casa Mio
19, Thatcher Close
Housing Area B10
Hereford

Dear Kimberly

If you are reading this then I'm sorry to say that something outrageous has happened to me and I'm laid up in my final LUP with no hope of exfil. Don't be too upset. It's an embuggerance but there you are. Shit happens. I only wish it didn't happen quite so often to me.

Look I know a lot of bad stuff happened between us in the past and I wasn't exactly an ideal husband to you in the week we had together. Though I probably didn't say so at the time I was well gutted when we split up. I know the least I should've done was give you an explanation but you know I've never been one for emotional stuff and... stuff. Believe me, abseiling off the roof and tabbing off down the road with the fish tank was the only way I could deal with it at the time. You're a smashing girl and deserved better than that — which is what I hear you're getting now three times a night from that bloke they call Donkey Dong who works in the motor pool.

Still whatever our ups and downs I want you to know that you really did mean the world to me and I will die with your name plastered all over my lips like so much mossie rep.

Yours, always,

Andy

Andy McGrabb

*Dear Side-Salad*
*Be a mate and*
*send a copy to each*
*of the 4 Kimberleys.*
*Their addresses are*
*in the rich tea biscuit*
*tin under the sink.*

PS  Sorry for blanking you in Sainsbury's that time but I was on a covert mission against a group of dangerous tea-bag counterfeiters and couldn't compromise my cover. Hope you understand!

PPS.  Say hello to your Mum for me.

X SQUADRON

22 SAS (AUXILIARY)

X Squadron
Special Air Service
Somewhere near Hereford
Herefordshire
HR1 SAS

Dear Ma and Pops

I'm sorry to inform you that I have apparently died. I am aware that this will come as something of a shock to you but rest assured that I gave my life in the line of duty, fighting for Queen and Country on some far-flung shore that will be forever England.

Bummer, eh? Still, I hope it doesn't come at too inconvenient a time for you, i.e. when you're packing up for Scotland and when Pippa's entered in the Gymkhana at Upper Slaughter.

If it's not too much trouble, I'd like to buried at St Bride's with full military honours. It would be nice if the vicar can keep his sermon short. As fascinating as his accounts of life in the African missions are to us, they might drag on a bit too long for outsiders. Furthermore, as there'll be so much 'Top Brass' there it would be a kindness if he didn't wear one of his floral dresses just this once. As for hymns, I think we could open the batting with 'Jerusalem', bring on 'I Vow To Thee My Country' as first change and lead the final run-chase with 'Swing Low, Sweet Chariot' – though you'll have to print up the words as everyone seems to know just the chorus.

Finally, let me thank you formally for being such jolly good parents. It really was very decent of you to bring me up, send me to a decent school and teach me to face life with my bat straight and my whites clean and pressed. I'm only sorry I won't be able to return the favour (for reasons beyond my control I should add!!).

Warmest wishes

Rupert

PS Can I be buried with Teddy as he really is a very silly bear and would get up to all sorts of mischief without me?

## Facsimile message

From: Mousse           To: Dear Sis           No. of Pages: 1

Hi. How you doin' ? Just a quick word about funeral arrangements. Look, we both know that Mum and Dad, though they both mean well, have about as much taste, as, well, anyone who still thinks Schrieber lounge units are the height of fashion. I'm depending on you to make sure nothing naff happens, to which end:

Music: Nothing religious or military. Think Massive Attack, think Orbital, think dub beats. If in doubt check what's really hot in The Face this week and play that.

Clothes: Don't let them bury me in uniform, unless it's the one I had taken in and restyled at Paul Smith at Christmas.

Coffin: Jasper Conran or if he's not free then maybe, just maybe Ted Baker. Of course, if Damien Hirst was up for it maybe we could do a see-through one with me suspended in formaldehyde, but maybe that's too, well, 1995 after all.

Food & Drink: Sushi and whatever bottled beer everyone's drinking in Soho this week.

Ciao for now.

PS Catholicism looks like it's coming back. If there's any chance of a requiem mass grab it with both hands.

http://www.sas.hereford.execution.com.uk

# X SQUADRON'S HOME PAGE ON THE WORLD-WIDE WEB

Hi. Welcome to the SAS home page. I'm Corporal Andy McGrabb MM DSM GPO of X Squadron (22 SAS) and I live in Hereford. My hobbies are slotting, publishing and flawed relationships.

Click here for how to get a book deal

Click here for 21 silent killing tips

Click here for today's recipe

Click here to detonate a small explosive charge beneath the work colleague of your choice

**Click here for details of our new tariffs for business users. Special discounts available this month on destabilising third-world economies and assassinating troublesome dictators**

Click here for tips on how to get in to the SAS, including details of the creative writing course

Think the SAS are a dangerously undemocratic bunch of thugs with no sense of respect for the Official Secrets Act and a predeliction for appearing on television? E-mail us here at sas.hereford.execution.com.uk giving your full name and address and details of your next of kin.

( – :

# PLANNING & INTELLIGENCE

## BY GENERAL SIR PETER DE LA BILLIONÈRE

IN MODERN WARFARE, nothing is more important than Planning & Intelligence. One cannot plan without intelligence, and one cannot be intelligent without planning. Many an operation has gone oboe-shaped due to the men planning to be intelligent and then failing to follow through with an intelligent plan.

Most of our intelligence comes from the Green Slime or spooks of the intelligence corps. These men are very experienced and exceedingly canny, and their ranks contain the highest number of pub trivia teams in the whole of the British Army. Many of them even went to school and can tie their own shoelaces with assistance and a manual.

They are of course, highly secretive and many of them still don't know their real identities. If someone calls out 'Hey, Bill' or 'What ho, Ted?' they often reply 'Yes?' in the hope that they may be mistaken for someone with a name. Their inability to sign cheques or open bank accounts has made them one of the cheapest sections of the British Army.

One famous intelligence officer of my acquaintance, Captain ____ became something of a legend when he changed his name by deed poll to Anon and received a plethora of literary awards for his poetry.

**The General showing the lads the location of the nearest Happy Eater.**

**'Inadequate planning and erroneous intelligence left Private Nobby Clarke seriously misled about the correct disguise for his infiltration of the Nuremberg Rally.'**

His Mother, Mrs ____ and his father, Brigadier ____ were very proud, as was their Dalmatian, ____.

But one has to be very specific with the intelligence chaps. Fact is, raw intelligence must be evaluated and sifted for useful material or you could end up in serious ____ with your ____ halfway up your ____ and no mistake.

For example, if you are undertaking a search and destroy mission in Central Asia, it's probably not that useful to be given the international dialling codes for the AA and instructions on how to operate a toilet in a Russian submarine. Whilst the pound/dinar exchange rate can be useful to a visiting tourist in Tunis, the exact location of the target at your location in Dar es Salaam is probably more pertinent to the fighting man.

Hence my experiences in Oman when I was sent upriver by the CO and found myself stranded in the desert carrying only a canoe and a small Welsh phrase book. Well and truly up *merde* creek *sans* paddle. Literally, in the case of the canoe. *Sans* river as well, in fact which wasn't in the plan, but that's intelligence for you.

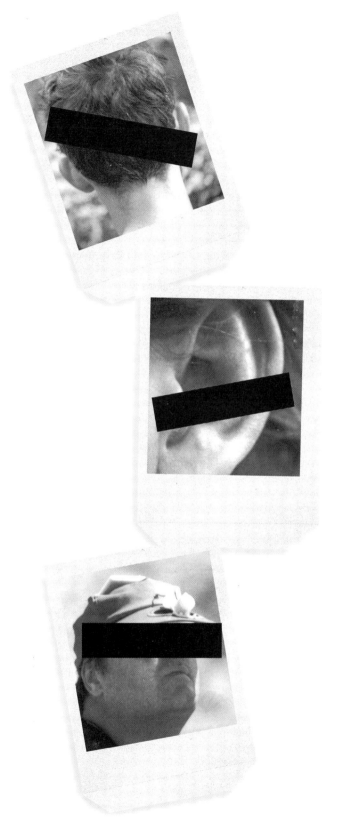

**Captain —— A legend.**

*T*he Navy boys say they won it, the Army lads take all the credit and the flash Harrys in their flying machines think it was all down to them. They're all wrong. We know who won it. The only difference is that we don't brag about it.

To be honest, before the shooting match went off I'd never even heard of the Falklands. Well, it's not the kind of place you go on holiday, is it? That all changed when the whole Regiment was ordered to gather at Hereford and told to start working on their wills. Word soon filtered down that Johnny Argie had stepped seriously out of line and it was up to us to teach him that Respect is spelt with a capital R. The Regiment, also spelt with a capital R, hadn't been massed like this since the beginning of the Second World War, and the atmosphere was even better than Abba at Wembley. We watched BBC1 – it was in the days before CNN – and waited for the big call-up. After a week only Side Salad, Mousse, Rupert, Scud, Fiji Bob and I were left sitting round the set. My big fear was that the war would be over before we got our chance; the Lego confiscated before we could lay the first brick.

I needn't have worried. It soon became apparent why we had been held back. Whereas the others had gone by boat, they were sending the Big Guys by air. Under cover of darkness we were spirited off to Stanstead where we boarded a plane which the untrained eye might have mistaken for your bog-standard charter flight to Tenerife. It was chock-a-block with people in convincing tourist gear talking about the weather. There was even the odd screaming baby to complete the effect.

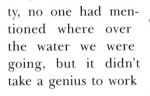

Boarding had been a doddle with just the one contact. It arose when a couple of uniformed Ruperts started gobbing off about us wanting to take our Bergens on as hand-luggage. Fiji Bob was the first to react with some textbook slotting. Quick, efficient and final – no one gains if you take your time over it.

Because of shortage of time, our mission statement had been necessarily brief. Go over the water, infiltrate, exfiltrate; or, to use the jargon, go over the water, infil, exfil. For reasons of security, no one had mentioned where over the water we were going, but it didn't take a genius to work

out that with Johnny Argie on the other side we were headed for B.A. – Buenos Aires. As he had seen *Evita* I made Side Salad 2 i/c which pissed off some of the others but you need someone who knows the territory as 2 i/c.

Fiji Bob was again the first to react, this time with a huge Eppie Scoppie. Muttering, 'This mission shite,' he bolted to the exit door, opened it in one swift movement and hurled himself off the plane. Unavoidably, a dozen so-called tourists were

sucked out after him. Let's hope, for their sakes, they'd packed their 'chutes in their hand luggage.

The first thing we noticed about Buenos Aires was that it is not so different from your average Spanish tourist resort. The place was overrun by sea-front bars, cheap hotels and pissed Jimmys. The second thing we noticed was that, considering there was a war going on, the locals were taking things very casually, lolling around and trying to sell cheap lighters. The third thing we noticed was that there were remarkably few, in fact no, pictures of Uncle Galtieri in the streets and bars.

This last observation really shocked me. Normally when you go behind enemy lines you can't move for pictures of the Oppo's Head Shed. But in Buenos Aires there was the odd poster advertising a Julio Iglesias concert and that was it. If we hadn't known better we could have been forgiven for thinking there wasn't a war going on.

After we had checked into our hotel, spent a few hours twisting by the pool and got some fresh inside ourselves, I called the men to order in Trish and Ray's El Lido bar. Not wanting to over complicate matters I decided that TR's should be the centre of operations. Scud was put on stag, Side Salad gave the kitchens a once-over, Mousse chatted to a sunburnt woman at the bar to pick up local info and Rupert told me a boring anecdote which ended with him getting a snog from his Spanish exchange. Before he could tell it to me again I ordered the team back to the hotel. There's no point overdoing things on the first night, especially when there's a war on.

Thank goodness for the good 'ol Currant Bun. Without the *Sun* we wouldn't have had a clue how the rest of the lads were getting on. Thanks to their excellent, unbiased reporting of events we were kept fully apprised of events. I don't know how they managed to fly 'em into Buenos Aires only a day after publication but it was worth it for the 'GOTCHA!' head-line alone. That really buoyed the lads' morale.

**It wasn't all fun and games in the Falklands. There was a war to be won.**

As a leader it falls to you to make the decisions. It comes with the territory. On day two I had to make the hardest decision of my life. Did we go ape-shit and take out as many Argies as we could, or did we do nothing? I had remembered from training the story of one of the heroes of the Regiment who had aborted his mission when he saw the flat, featureless terrain which made his aims impossible. Rather than senselessly go on he had taken his men back to the chopper and returned to base.

Some people questioned his integrity but I personally consider it to be one of the bravest acts of any war. I'm glad to say I'm made of the same stuff. After a continental breakfast, stale croissants, no jam, I solemnly marched the men back to the airport from whence we had come.

Back in Hereford the debriefing was one of the quickest I can remember. It was generally agreed that we had acheived what we had set out to do. And no one can ask more than that. From early on I have realised that it is remarkably difficult to pinpoint what exactly constitutes 'a good war'. Is it how many foreigners you kill? Is it how many Brits you save? Is it being part of the team? There are no easy answers to these deeply philosophical questions but, for what it's worth, my view is that a good war is one in which you do your bit. We had done our bit. If we hadn't, the war might have gone the other way. History, itself, might have been very different. No wonder Maggie was thankful. No wonder so many of us responded to her gratitude by voting for her in '87. It was the least we could do.

**Only a fool would continue a mission when faced with such flat, featureless terrain.**

*Cometh the hour, cometh the man. The buck stops here. No one remembers who finished second. Take it to the top. It was an operational fuck-up, not a ministeri-al one. All these handy phrases revolve around the concept of leadership. And, when one studies one's history books, it is the leaders that stand out and grab the attention. Who, for instance, can name William the Conqueror's 2 i/c at the Battle of Hastings, or, indeed, Christopher Columbus's Scaley? No one, I'd wager. I, quite simply, am a leader. And therefore handily placed to pass on a few tips on that knottiest of problems – what makes a great leader?*

'Speak softly and carry a big stick' said Theodore Roosevelt. 'A little whippy willow one can also be fun' said General De La Billionère.

## IT CAN'T BE TAUGHT

Leaders are born, not made; bred, not manufac-tured; nannied, not mothered. Sensibly, the British have cottoned on to this essential truth and set up an educational system that reflects this fact. Leaders are educated at some expense at a school with a history of leadership, surrounded by people of the right kidney. Others, or should I say non-leaders in these politically correct times, are not.

Having made this distinction at an early stage, sorted out the wheat from the chaff as it were, the British, again sensibly, do all they can to ensure it holds good for the rest of one's life. Imagine the administrative headaches that would ensue if non-leaders suddenly came over all uppity and attempt-ed to become leaders – total, bloody nightmare.

## A BIT OF ARROGANCE
## NEVER HURT ANYBODY

Goes without saying, but, perversely, often has to be said. The one quality that marks out a leader from his fellow men is an ability to rise effortlessly above them and smartly put them in their place. Naturally, this sometimes doesn't go down well. I've lost count of the number of times one member of my troop has resorted to violence after I've casually remarked, 'Scud, remind me again, which house were you in at Eton?'

## IT'S MAKING THE DECISION THAT COUNTS, NOT WHETHER IT'S RIGHT OR WRONG

From the moment that, as a prefect, you have to make your first decision, whether to order Stubbs to run round the school grounds backwards, or, despite the extra paperwork, simply expel him, you realise the essential truth of this maxim. The backwards run might do Stubbs some good, expulsion might benefit the school, it's a tough one to call. However, if you get into a dither and start weighing up the pros and cons it will be harmful to you, the school and, most particularly, to Stubbs. As anyone who has ever visited a dentist is well aware, it is the waiting that hurts. So, for Stubbs' sake, make your mind up quickly.

Likewise, if on a mission the compass goes on the blink it is vital that the leader makes a decision sharpish. After all, you may be going in the wrong direction but at least you'll all know where you're going.

**A good leader ensures that his squadron have access to the best facilities in the field.**

### COUP D'ÉTATS

'Meet the new boss, same as the old boss', Peter Townshend, as prescient as usual, once delightfully sang. How very true, Peter, and it's this factor which ensures that Britain remains the only country with a 'Great' in front of its name. It is the continuity in the leadership which helps explain our continued success.

When the knives come out and it becomes apparent that it might be in my best interests to stand down, I will choose my successor with care – first port of call being the immediate family. Any relative over eighteen not wearing an earring gets the job. If that port proves to be dry, then I will move on to a list supplied by the Old Etonian Association which conveniently names everyone who attended the school. Finally, as a port of last resort, I will throw into the hat anyone who has ever invited me to their country house for the weekend.

**Chastisement. A man respects a general with a firm grip.**

# COVER STORIES

## By Andy McGrabb

**W**hen you're taken captive by a bunch of jundies, the only thing that is going to stop them whipping out their chutney ferrets and giving you it up the chocolate speedway is a damn good cover story. Their importance, therefore, cannot be overestimated. The ideal cover story should be clear, concise, believable and, above all, interesting. The last thing you want is for the jundies to start getting bored and their minds turning to other things.

## NUMBERS

Make sure the numbers in your cover story correspond to the number of people in your troop. Sounds obvious but you'd be amazed at how often even crack members of the troop overlook the bleeding obvious. I've seen a gang of six hanging out in the Belize area pretending to be on a seven-a-side Rugby tour and five blokes tabbing round Africa togged up as the Three Amigos.

So get the numbers right or, even better, come up with a cover story which involves flexible numbers (e.g. is your average jundie going to know how many people make up a regulation morris dancing team?).

## CLARITY

Crucial. Everyone on your mission must be able to retell the story at the drop of hat, or trouser belt, and years of attempting to pass off other people's war stories as my own have taught me to KISS (keep it simple stupid). The story should be stripped to its bare essentials and left at that. Ideally, it should consist of the three acts listed opposite.

## Act One:

Introduce the characters but don't fill in too many of the details. Allow the audience a chance to think for themselves.

## Act Two:

Move the plot along a bit and end with your central character – yourself – facing up to a helluva dilemma.

## Act Three:

Resolve the dilemma and tag on a happy ending.

**The gear is convincing, but how many central Africans have seen *The Three Amigos*?**

# BELIEVABILITY

At the end of the day it all boils down to the way you tell them. Some people are natural-born storytellers; some people get flustered, go red in the face and start stammering uncontrollably. If you fall into the latter camp, there is little you can do but play dumb and brush up your skills as a mime.

However good a bullshitter you are, it still helps if you employ a bit of common sense. Even a bone-stupid Bolivian is not going to believe you if you start claiming you are on a school geography trip which has gone horribly wrong. Equally, your most backward Afghan is unlikely to fall for the old stag-night routine. The best thing to pretend to be is a doctor. Everybody respects and loves doctors. Sure, you often wind up doing a bit of impromptu surgery on an unfortunate local, but it's a small price to pay, and let's face it, it's the unfortunate local who's paying it.

# BE INTERESTING

Not as easy as it looks, whole books have been devoted to this subject and yet we are still no nearer an answer. The easiest mistake to make is to think you're being interesting when in fact you're boring the arse off everyone. Obviously, in certain situations, such as when you're paying for the meal, you can get away with this, but when you've been taken captive at someone else's expense the boot is very definitely on the other foot. And more likely than not to end up in your mouth.

One handy tip is that people are more likely to find you interesting if you are self-deprecating rather than boastful. Essentially, people prefer hearing how crap you are rather than how great you are, as it makes them feel better. It's called human nature (e.g. if you are running with the Morris Dancers gambit it would be preferable to embellish your cover story with an anecdote about how you fucked up rather than one in which you danced faultlessly, won all the medals going and drank the opposition under the table in the pub afterwards.)

# MOUSSE'S GUIDE TO
# STYLISH
## ANONYMITY

When you're in a top secret crack organisation like the Regiment, maintaining your anonymity is as much a part of your job as slotting foreigners or appearing in your own hit TV show. The way most of us do this is the old Thin Black Line Over The Eyes Technique or TBLOTET for short. After a while this can get a little boring, so why not spice up your low profile by using some of my own innovative suggestions?

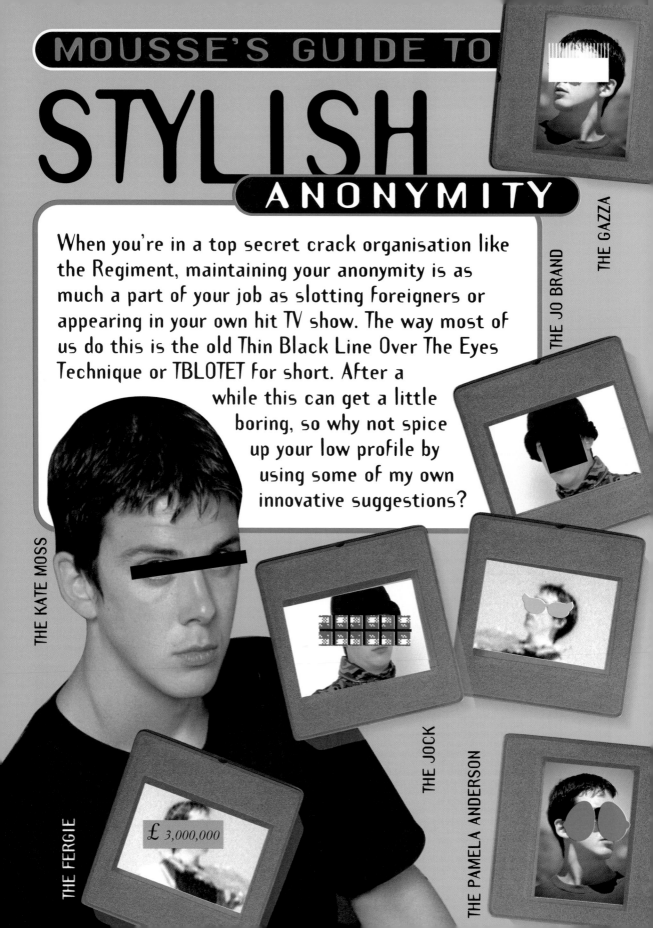

THE GAZZA

THE JO BRAND

THE KATE MOSS

THE JOCK

THE PAMELA ANDERSON

THE FERGIE

£ 3,000,000

# The Doo-Bee-Doo-Bee-Doo Incident — 1963

The First Lady demonstrating the infamous 'Jackie O' hand shuffle.

The Regiment has attracted its fair share of celebrity afficionados and X Squadron is no exception. In the 1960s, when on secondment to the CIA Covert Beatnik Annihilation Force, the Squadron were befriended by popular crooner Frank Sinatra. After losing a game of poker to Jackie Kennedy, Sinatra found that the First Lady had been playing with a marked deck, and during an all-night drinking session asked the squadron to 'put the frighteners on her'. He suggested a regimental sharpshooter should shoot off her hat during a presidential trip to Dallas. Tragically, the task was assigned to X Squadron's Sergeant 'Speccy' McGurk and the rest is history – and subject to the little-known 100-year Restricted Information Act.

SARGEANT 'SPECCY' McGURK, NOW LIVING IN ARGENTINA.

# KILLING HOUSE

*A*t Hereford we have a place called the Killing House. A sort of permanent training environment that contains all sorts of hazards and perils such as cardboard cut-outs that leap out at you, mined wardrobes, Anthea Turner and those low coffee tables that really do your shins in when you bump into them in the dark. It's a bit of a tradition for government ministers, VIPs and Royals to visit us here during training so that they can be well prepared if they are ever kidnapped and liberated by the Regiment. My job is to keep a sort of scorecard of their reactions whilst 17 armed men burst through the windows firing live rounds. I love my job.

### JEREMY BEADLE
**REACTIONS:**

The recorded highlights of what Rupert calls 'Mr Beadle's involuntary bowel movements' are now available on video.

**FACIAL EXPRESSION:**

If you put him on rewind he sucks up his own vomit and his face turns from blue to green to a really healthy pink, although the grin is a bit forced.

**BROWN TROUSER RATING: 12**

## JEFFREY ARCHER
**REACTIONS:**

As so often, first indications were good as the subject told us he had once been in the parachute regiment and had taken out a foxhole of the Boche on his own. He mentioned that he was related to Field Marshal Montgomery and lived in the house of a noted war poet which made him incapable of fear. Also that he wasn't just a well-known novelist but had, for years, been a secret agent for MI5. He showed us his special code ring which looked very much like the ones they gave away with Rice Crispies in 1971. He didn't actually get into the Killing House as we done his legs in the car park. It was the only way we could shut him up.

**FACIAL EXPRESSION:**
Smug with just a hint of ingratiating chumminess.

**BROWN TROUSER RATING: 0**
People like this are too stupid to be afraid.

# HIS ROYAL HIGHNESS PRINCE EDWARD

### REACTIONS:

Again first indications were good as he seemed to be making a call on his mobile phone when we locked him in. He remained cool when the lights went out although he did slip his thumb into his mouth. The cardboard cut-out of Andrew Lloyd Webber got a bit of a shiver out of him, but this was soon overtaken by a sort of high-pitched squeaking noise when the theatrical impresario disintegrated in a hail of tracer. The grenades we threw down his strides may have shaken him a bit, but he was soon laughing along with the rest of us when we pointed out that the pins were still in. At least I think it was laughter. Sort of choking noise through the nose anyway.

### FACIAL EXPRESSION:

Startled faun

**BROWN TROUSER RATING: 8**

# DUCHESS OF YORK SARAH FERGUSON

### REACTIONS:

Our condolences go out to her financial advisers and the Regiment very much regrets the turn of events. Sometimes you just have to give in to your instincts.

### FACIAL EXPRESSION:

Tanned at first, then paler with flecks of shrapnel.

### BROWN TROUSER RATING:

She wouldn't be seen dead in anything as tasteful as brown trousers. In fact when we helped her into the ambulance, she was wearing a chartreuse puffball evening gown with purple shoes and a selection of matching field dressings.

# MARGARET THATCHER

### REACTIONS:

Mags is down here every weekend of course, so she is well used to it by now. She didn't bat an eye when

we put forty rounds into the sideboard she was leaning on and the grenades only wrinkled her tights. But the key to good training is finding their weak spot, so we handed Ted Heath a Minimi and gave her a ten second head start. You'd be surprised how fast she can shift in a pair of heels.

### FACIAL EXPRESSION:

Same as always, although something's happened behind the eyes and with the sagging neck she's beginning to look like a deranged turkey. Still a game old bird though, and the lads definitely agree with Alan Clark. This woman is pure sex when she's on the warpath and it's worth mentioning John Major just to see her veins pop out.

**BROWN TROUSER RATING: -34**

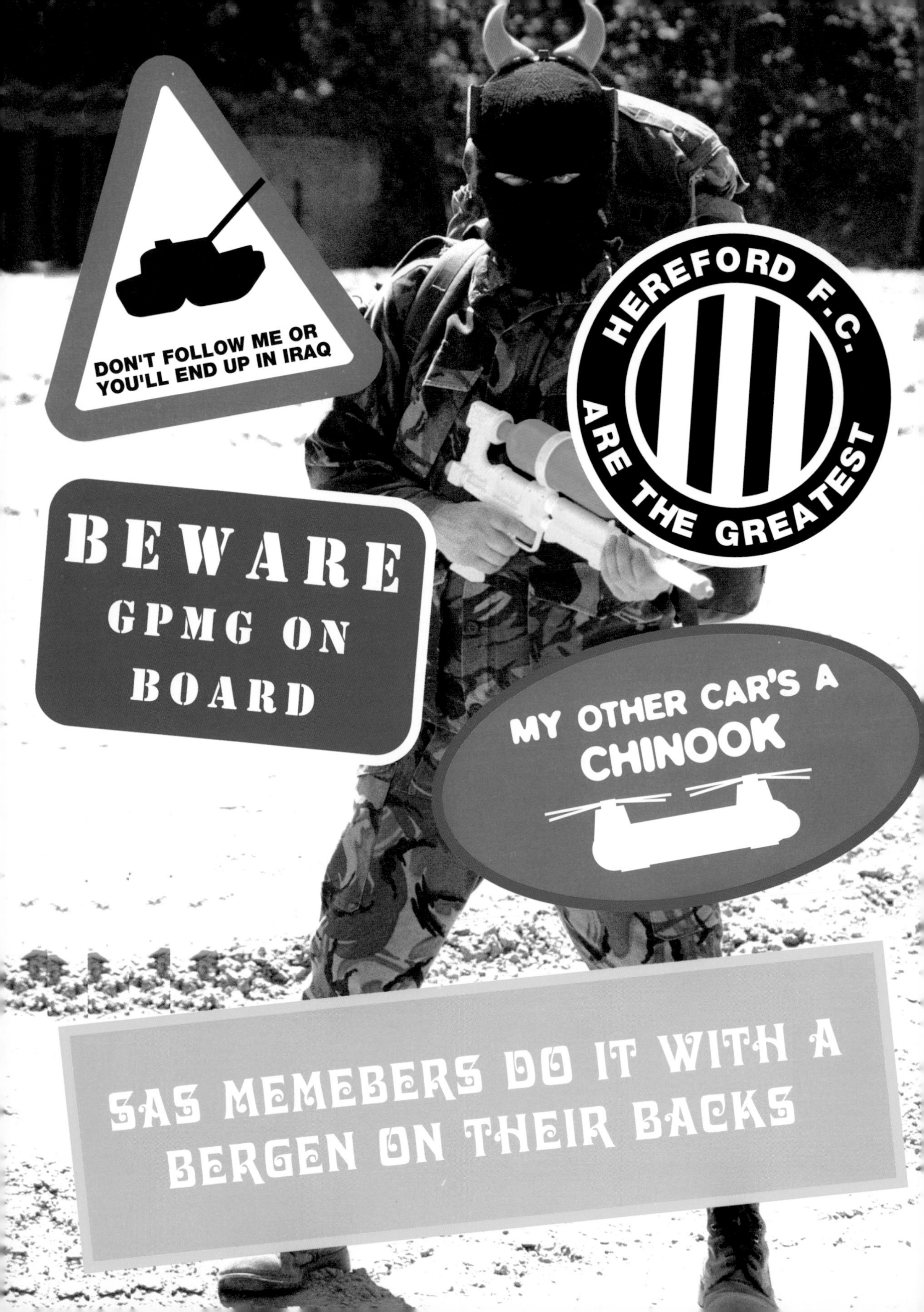
DON'T FOLLOW ME OR
YOU'LL END UP IN IRAQ
HEREFORD F.C.
ARE THE GREATEST
BEWARE
GPMG ON
BOARD
MY OTHER CAR'S A
CHINOOK
SAS MEMEBERS DO IT WITH A
BERGEN ON THEIR BACKS

# MAGIC EYE

It was once said that to be a really effective soldier in the Regiment you had to have eyes that can see things that other men blink at. This is truer than words can say. To help us attain this level of visual perfection we in

X Squadron have devised a number of our own unique top-secret tests – a couple of which we're reproducing now for your reading pleasure. Study this apparently random pattern carefully. Can you see the real picture beneath?

Answer: Actually it's a bit embarrassing. This is a picture one of Scud's kids drew for his birthday. Still, it will probably look nice up on the wall in the kitchen.

# Fiji Bob's Astrological Guide to the Fijian Zodiac

## Fiji Bob's STARS

### Heckler & Kochalam
#### SEP 22–OCT 22

The heavenly twins, Heckler & Kochalam are explosive characters whose tempers are rarely under control. They eat nails and shit bullets, which can be hazardous if you're sharing their tent. Their principal ambition in life is to face 20,000 IRA men armed only with a sharp stick and a ring pull, before expiring in a hail of gunfire screaming 'Millwall for the Cup' in the company of the very lovely Miss Sinead O'Connor and Miss Michael Portillo. They enjoy Laura Ashley soft furnishings, long summer afternoons punting up the Grand Union Canal in a midget submarine and the hopping scene in *Truly, Madly, Deeply*.

**THIS WEEK**
On Monday you will be asked to appear in a reconstruction of the Iranian Embassy Siege for a major ITV documentary. You will do this again for the BBC on Tuesday, for CBS on Wednesday, for HBO on Thursday and for the Open University module on gratuitous TV violence on Friday. Saturday you will be interviewed by *World In Action* and forced to admit that during the actual Iranian Embassy Siege you were at home in Pinner grouting the downstairs bathroom.

Lucky Sandwich: Cordite
Lucky after shave: 'Obsession'

## Fiji Bob's STARS

### Billieregalam
#### JUNE 21–JULY 21

BILLIEREGALAMS are mercurial father figures with lantern jaws and dubious pretensions. In the presence of their superiors (Americans) they are prone to impulsive gestures and rash decisions. (i.e., 'Let's bomb some fleeing conscripts until they're a small stain on the road.') They are apt to claim massive victories and great strategic advantage simply by going to the chemists. Billieregalams enjoy holidays in the Algarve, pointing at maps and wearing berets.

**THIS WEEK**
An emu farm investment in Siberia will collapse beneath a glacier with your money inside it early in the week, and you will be forced to pen tedious memoirs with muscular titles about your brilliant and highly secret military career, your annoying Aunt Joyce and your nagging lower back pain. On Wednesday your investment in an Alaskan fridge/freezer centre may prove financially embarassing and you will be forced to take up a post with a major merchant bank, despite knowing almost as much about banking as you do about selling frozen emus. Later in the week you will be fired for strafing three customers who exceed their overdraft limit.

Lucky sandwich: Emu
Lucky after shave: 'Testosterone pour homme'

## Fiji Bob's STARS

### Clintonalam
#### NOV 21–DEC 20

CLINTONALAMS are subject to sudden attacks of tiredness lasting from five to ten years. Their eyes sometimes disappear into their pudgy little faces and their voices can take on the quality of Marianne Faithful's after a hard night shagging with the chief executive of the Mars Corporation. In the presence of impending elections they are apt to launch vote winning attacks on Arab nations.

**THIS WEEK**
Venus lowering will see past mistakes returning to haunt you. On Monday you will appear before the Grand Jury to answer questions relating to your priapic electioneering methods and your wife's ability to shred documents with her stilettos. You will escape conviction by fondling the breasts of the chief prosecutor, the clerk and the jury foreman. Tuesday, Wednesday, Thursday and Friday will see you in court again over the three sexual harassment charges arising from Monday's events.

Lucky sandwich: Stripped cheerleader with no dressing and mayo on the side. Hold the onions.
Lucky after shave: Whitewater rafter with a hint of fraud.

## Fiji Bob's STARS

### SaddamalamwohoBlackBettywalam
#### JAN 20–FEB 18

SADDAMALAMWOHOBLACKBETTYWAMALAMS are whimsical and fey with a strong creative streak. They are fond of small furry animals and gassing civilians. They are quick to make friends, particularly with those who are willing to give them the occasional tank battalion or air force, although they often feel betrayed by former close friends who train them to use Scud missiles and then bomb them when they do. They enjoy cutting off the extremities of close relatives, refusing to die and wearing comedy eyebrows.

**THIS WEEK**
The close proximity of Jupiter to your opposing sign of mayhem may mean some surprises early in the week with a minor coup or small manicuring accident in the offing. Thursday will see a United Nations Weapons Inspection falling into a large crack in your underground nuclear weapons establishment. Friday will be spent ringing Margaret Thatcher and George Bush yelling 'I'm still here and you're drawing pensions. Who won the war then eh?' When they refuse to come to the 'phone, you will stand on the Israeli border yelling 'It's all gone quiet over there'.

Lucky sandwich: Sheep in a bap
Lucky after shave: Not applicable. Don't actually shave.

# SCUD'S
## TOP TIPS

Tabbing across 150 miles of Welsh hills without a toilet break is tough on the feet. Here's a tip for protecting those precious plates. In the chemists they sell these dead good foot pads called Bodyform or Kotex. If you put one in your boots you can protect the soles of your feet on those long route marches. If you get the ones with wings, you can also cushion your instep.

Another genuine SAS survival tip – guaranteed for life

# Love and marriage

Let's face it. Keeping down a job and a relationship is hard enough at the best of times for most people these days. When you're in the Regiment it's infinitely more hard – if not harder.

Think about it. Top-quality soldiering like ours involves total commitment 24 hours a day, 365 days a year, year in, year out. Missions, training, having lunch with your publisher – it's work, work, work in X Squadron. As much as you enjoy it, you can't help noticing that you pay a heavy price when it comes to your inter-personal relationships – which in my case works out at around 22 grand a year in maintenance payments and legal fees.

Still, a man has his needs and not all of them can be met by a shiny new piece of kit or a six-month surveillance job in Honolulu. Birds inevitably come into the picture somewhere and it's a rare man indeed who goes through his whole career in the Regiment without some sort of 'Close Quarter Contact with Special Forces of a Gentler Kind'. How this works out for you – like any other fire-fight – is all a question of planning, personal preparation and ruthless professionalism on the day.

KIMBERLEY I

## MEETING BIRDS

Make no mistake. Birds like a man in uniform – not just any uniform obviously, or traffic wardens would be going round with big smiles on their faces – no, real military uniforms. To birds they represent all kinds of deep female wants and desires: danger, romance, index-linked widows' pensions.

KIMBERLEY II

Of course this presents a bit of a problem if you happen to be in a top-secret regiment with a big thing about hiding its identity from members of the general public. How can you capitalise on the Soldier Factor without giving the game away to what could, after all, be just a lure planted by the enemy to make you break cover? The answer of course is to have a strategy.

Picture the scene. You're in the Scud & Sixpence in Hereford enjoying a quiet bare knuckle fight with your mates. You look up and see a gorgeous bird at the bar giving you that special look which, if they bottled it, would have the words 'Pure Animal Lust' on the label. You stagger towards her and, trying not to bleed on her white stilettos, initiate a contact.

You: *Alright, darling?*
Bird: *Yeah. You in the Regiment then?*
You: *Me? Nah. I'm a multimillionaire who's desperate to have kids.*
Bird: (WALKING AWAY) *Oh. That's a shame. I only knob soldiers.*
You: (PANICKING) *Actually, now you come to mention it...*

Well, it's a kind of strategy... as I told the court martial on several occasions, the truth is they are gonna find out eventually so why not lay it on the line right up front, before you invest heavily in flowers and clean underwear?

## MARRYING THEM

Well, you've got to, haven't you? At least I know I do. And do and do and do. After all, when you're dealing in life and death every day, as we do in the Regiment, you begin to get a bit of a sense what the Great Head Shed in the sky had in mind when he issued the human race its battle orders. Get born, grow up, find a nice girl, settle down, build several types of fixed and flexible shelving... and piss off abroad for months on end shooting people. You know it makes sense in the end.

Getting hitched, though, is still no laughing matter. In fact, as anyone who's ever met any of my four ex-wives will tell you, it's deadly serious. To this end I've compiled a special check-list of Do's and Don'ts that I run myself through every time I make a life-long commitment.

KIMBERLEY III

## DO'S AND DON'TS

### DO

Remember the bride's proper name. Nicknames like 'Fart Face' and 'The Camel' are all very well among mates in the Regimental bar but tend to go down poorly if used in the groom's speech. If in doubt you can have it tattooed discreetly on your hand, though if everything goes pear-shaped this does mean you'll have to do what I did and marry someone else with the same name.

• Reveal the wedding location in advance to your guests. It's not everyone's idea of a good time to be given a blank piece of paper marked 'Wedding' and told to figure out the rest for themselves. If you are going to organise transport, try to make it appropriate to the situation. As much as you may think it normal to go from the church to the reception in the loading bay of a Hercules, your bride may have other ideas.

### DON'T

• Abseil into the church unless you really, really have to. Though obviously it can make for a nice dramatic opening to the ceremony, the stun grenades will play havoc with some of the older relatives and you'll only upset the vicar if you make a hole in his new roof.

• Get married in full black kit. OK, you'll look the dog's bollocks in the photo's but you'll spend years picking bits of confetti out of your Bergen.

KIMBERLEY IV...

### DIVORCE

Shit happens. The best laid plans can go awry. Fire-fights are lost. As with any other military reverse, the secret of a good divorce is all in the exfil. These are the rules I've learnt from bitter experience:

• Get a good cover story and stick to it. There's nothing that frustrates an enemy interrogator more than a complete load of bollocks repeated over and over again. Of course you know that she knows that what you were doing with her best friend in the woodshed had nothing to do with first aid, but you're generally protected under international conventions until you break cover and actually admit it.

• If that fails to work and she starts to attack you with kitchen implements, then get the hell out of there a.s.a.p. Don't hesitate, don't explain. Just say 'I'll see ya' doll. Its been huge fun', find the nearest third-floor window and leap out. I think you'll find she'll actually be quite impressed, in a seething, hate-filled kind of a way.

• Never go back to retrieve pieces of kit. However vital they may seem at the time, the enemy is bound to use this opportunity to attack you again. Obviously this doesn't apply to kit belonging to your new girlfriend, which you must rescue without any thought of personal safety.

• Go back to base, dress your wounds, debrief the lads on what went wrong, have a laugh about it, go down the Scud & Sixpence for a few beers, get into a quiet bare knuckle fight... and start the whole thing over again.

Mrs. Nan Pryce,
13 Misery Lane,
Cwmglum,
Dyfed,
Wales.

Dear Nan,

Who'd have thought when I was back home dreaming of travelling to cosmopolitan Pontypridd for a glamorous night in the Wimpy bar that one day I'd be here in the Burmese jungle? We have been out of food and water for seven days so I haven't had much of a chance to do any cooking up till today. Then Rory had a ND (Negligent Discharge) which was very messy and needed a special solvent to get the stains out of the hammock. He also fired his weapon by mistake and shot our Sargeant, Jock 'Bastard' Mc Sondheim.

It was the catering triumph of this whole tour, Nan. I started off thinking simple, just basting him in a coconut and lemon grass marinade and wrapping his sweetbreads in a banana leaf, before searing him on both sides. But then I thought, 'Oh bugger. It's not every day you get to eat a commanding officer. Let's go all the way. Five hours later I'd got him boned and rolled in a raspberry coulis on a bed of kiwi puree. Luckily Rory's stray bullet also shot off Fiji Bob's remaining toes, so we had them as an entree with a very nice Chateau Lafite I'd been keeping in my water bottle. The lads were a bit narked when I decanted it actually. Apparently they'd all been drinking swamp water for two weeks.

Love to the cat.

All the best,

Harry.

FAITHFUL UNTO D'EATH

Sir Richard & Lady D'eath Cutie,
Haemoglobin Hall,
Little Dorrit,
Wiltshire,
Blighty,

Dear Ma and Pops

Covert ops are as bloody as I Imagined. However, one musn't grumble about the provisions. Today the Welsh private in our team really did us proud at brunch with several quarters of some local venison which one of the chaps must have caught in some dreadfully ingenious snare. I'm a little concerned about 'Side-Salads' personal hygiene though, as I did lose lose a tooth on a signet ring that I found amongst the breaded goujons we had as an entree.

I am very worried about our Sergeant. He went off into the bush to beat a path through the undergrowth and never returned. Andy said he'd 'gone home for some clean pants'. I do think it irresponsible that a commanding officer should so readily abandon his charges to the rigours of covert ops simply because he wanted to alter his trousering.

Must dash now it is nearly supper and Private Pryce is sautee-ing some Meatballs. At least I think they're meatballs.

Rupert
D'eath-Cutie

**MOUSSE MCCRACKEN**
**HEIGHT** 6.0
**EYE COLOUR** BLUE
**HAIR** DARK BROWN
**SHOE SIZE** 8
**MODEL AGENCY** SAS

Mr George Hamilton
Melanoma Mansion
Beverley Hills
Hollywood, California

Dear Mr Hamilton

I am a British soldier on covert ops in the Burmese jungle where temperatures can reach 115° in the shade and thought someone of your experience might be able to help me out. How do you get an even tan under tree cover? Your skin colour is always the right side of fashionable ochre and I know you could give me a tip or two.

Of course I know you're really busy with your film career. Well done on your stunning performance in that TV movie about the woman who decapitated too deeply and spent the rest of the film saying goodbye to her family from a water bed in Cedars Sinai Intensive Care. It was a cautionary ~~tale~~ lesson for all of us who take effective excess hair removal for granted.

*Mousse*

P.S What's your position on chest waxing?

---

**Threshers Off License**
**Brewery Road**
**Jarrow**
Dear Sanjit — Please send a crate of Special Brew and some of them ice beers you charge a chuffing fortune for. I want a box of crisps, 5 crispy bacon, 4 salt & vinegar, 2 cheese & onion and 2 hedgehog. Also nip next door to the Patel Grocery and pick up some limes for Mousse to put in the neck of the bottle. Send the lot to 'Scud' 22 SAS, Burma, WI and hurry up. I'm bloody gasping here. Don't cock this up Sanjit — I'll send you a postal order next month.

**Scud**

X SQUADRON

22 SAS (AUXILIARY)

Kimberley the III
Dunbloodletting
19 Tebbit Drive
Housing Area E13
Hereford


Dear Kimberley,
Go to the cupboard under the sink and get out that stain devil for
bloodstains we got from the chemist when I turbocharged the lawn
mower. Then write on a clean piece of paper (use gloves), 'I'm
really sorry about Sergeant McSondheim but I just couldn't take it
anymore. He was outrageous and in the end I just had to get rid
of the embuggerance.' Sign it Fiji Bob and post it to Hereford
Murder Squad.

Then book a one-way ticket to Hackney Downs, pack a bag with
everything you have and lock the house after you. Leave the keys
under the mat. I'm sorry mate, but I think it's for the best. You
were getting too possessive and one thing I can't have is anyone
ordering me about and telling me what to do.

See you mate


Andy

Andy

PS Your one good move was to tidy up the house and buy a dinner
service. I'll never forget that. Here's looking at you, Kid. We'll
always have Pyrex.

## X SQUADRON

# The Falklands Campaign

The Falklands War has been described by some greasy foreigner as 'two bald men fighting over a comb'. The Regiment has always maintained that a good comb can also be used to comb lice out of your uniform and serves as a useful prop for Hitler impressions. It is thus well worth fighting for.

Anyway, despite the casualties and loss of life, the war was a pretty good bet. The Regiment had learnt a powerful lesson from the American defeat in Vietnam. Never, ever get into a war with highly

TEENAGE ENEMY CONSCRIPT
PREPARING TO ATTACK

O'CALLAGHAN. TWICE THE MAN YOU ARE

trained enemy soldiers. The Falklands and Gulf Wars were both distinguished by large numbers of teenage enemy conscripts who ran away a lot and weren't quite sure about the trigger thingy on their weapons. The Falklands Campaign, as everyone knows, was absolutely necessary to protect a vital resource that would have disappeared without it. And she has certainly shown her appreciation since by sending us a Harrod's hamper every year signed 'To My Darling Little Election Winners. Love Mags'. A legendary figure in X Squadron was Johnny 'Two Pairs' O'Callaghan, the subject of a ribald song amongst the men that went ' One ball abnormal, two balls normal, three balls Superman, four balls – O'Callaghan'. It was he who led the charge against over 200 of the enemy at Puffin Meadow. Miraculously there was only one casualty when one of the lead ewes sank her teeth into my swagger stick. I am proud to say that it still bears the marks to this day.

# Fiji Bob's Astrological Guide to the Fijian Zodiac

## Fiji Bob's STARS

## Thatcheralamalam

### APRIL 19–MAY 19

THATCHERALAMALAM is a whisky sign and bears some comparison with its sister sign of Saddamalamwohoblackbettywamalam. They are often found beneath tables at social events, singing 'Simply The Best' and dribbling on their son's hush puppies. They rarely make much sense after opening time and may take chunks out of your lower limbs if left unmuzzled. They enjoy Barry Manilow, cirrhosis of the liver and BSE cheeseburgers.

### THIS WEEK

Monday will see you at Guys Hospital having a Portillo surgically removed from your left leg and an early appointment with the proctologist to remove the John Selwyn Gummer. Wednesday will see you visiting your favourite regiment and idling away a few hours reminiscing and planning a mortar attack on Downing Street. Friday will be a difficult day as you struggle to escape the two white-coated men with the jacket that does up the back. You will probably put them into traction before sighing, 'My name is Blanche. Blanche Dubois. It means white woods.'

Lucky sandwich: Argie with mayo
Lucky after shave: 'Brut'

---

## Fiji Bob's STARS

 ## Schwarzkopf

### JULY 22–AUG 21

SCHWARZKOPFS are generally bull-necked dullards who revel in phrases like 'non-affirmative interlocutory response' or 'no' as it's sometimes pronounced by people with normal haircuts. Schwarzkopfs have been generally irritable since they discovered that their star sign also means 'blackhead' in German. They are often found shouting 'Gee, was that your tank? Golly we're sorry, it looked so like the Iraqi Republican Guard in a Volvo' in an impressive basso rumble reminiscent of Orson Welles on the toilet. They are fond of uniforms two sizes too small for their gut, missiles with video cameras and collateral damage.

### THIS WEEK

On Monday you will be decorated for your military efforts to maintain the stability of Government. On Tuesday you will discover that the Government in question was Iraq's. On Wednesday you will be tied up, interrogated, whipped and tortured. Your lunch with Miss Demeanour over, you will return to the office. Friday will be a difficult day as you struggle to complete the latest volume of your memoirs. 'Sitting on My Ass while the SAS Did All the Work'.

Lucky sandwich: Bullshit Burger with balls on the side
Lucky after shave: 'Napalm Melody' by Colonel Sanders. 'It's whisker lickin' good'.

---

## STARS

 ## MajorMajor

### OCT 23–NOV 21

MAJORMAJORs are generally placid woodland creatures with a soft underbelly frequently harassed by their opposing sign of Thatcheralam. Prone to nasal dysfunction, Majormajors are often reduced to a monotonous drone. Sometimes found sticking out of a tank hatch wearing a sandy jumper with elbow patches and ear muffs, looking for all the world like a misplaced tobacconist. They are fond of cricket, gnomes and liberated older women.

### THIS WEEK

On Wednesday you will go to the Houses of Parliament for an exchange of nasal non sequiturs delivered by suburban grammar school boys. At 3.30 you will get bored and the conkers will come out. At 4.00 Norman Lamont will shout 'The Prime Minister may have a good point to make about the economy, but he's only got a sixer and his mum worked in Sainsbury's.'

Lucky sandwich: Fish paste with the crusts cut off by Norma
Lucky after shave: 'Denim for PM's' – Sainsbury's own

---

## STARS

 ## Koowaytees

### FEB 19–MAR 19

There are two types of KOOWAYTEES. Those with no vote and those in royal families. The latter version are well dressed and likely to be in possession of gold bidets. The former are liable to develop death or long prison sentences for having a transistor radio. KOOWAYTEES are full of promise. Every year they promise elections and every year they get other KOOWAYTEES to promise to forget. KOOWAYTEES are fond of sand in their shamags, money resting snugly in their pockets next to large western governments and substantial oil revenues.

### THIS WEEK

Your country will be invaded early in the week but returned to you in small pieces within a year. Generous white eyes will offer to put it all back together again for only 20 squillion dinar and the recipe for couscous.

Lucky sandwich: Krugerrand Baguette
Lucky after shave: 'Winds of the Desert' by The American Suppository Company Inc.

REGIMENTAL PIN-UP

# HELLO BOYS

OR ARE YOU JUST PLEASED TO SEE ME?

COMBAT

# FIELD SIGNALS

**TENSIONS HAVE DEVELOPED IN PATROL, PLEASE SEND THERAPIST**

**TENSIONS HAVE BEEN RESOLVED, PLEASE SEND FLOWERS**

**ENEMY SIGHTED, PLEASE EXFIL NOW**

**LAGER SUPPLIES ARE LOW**

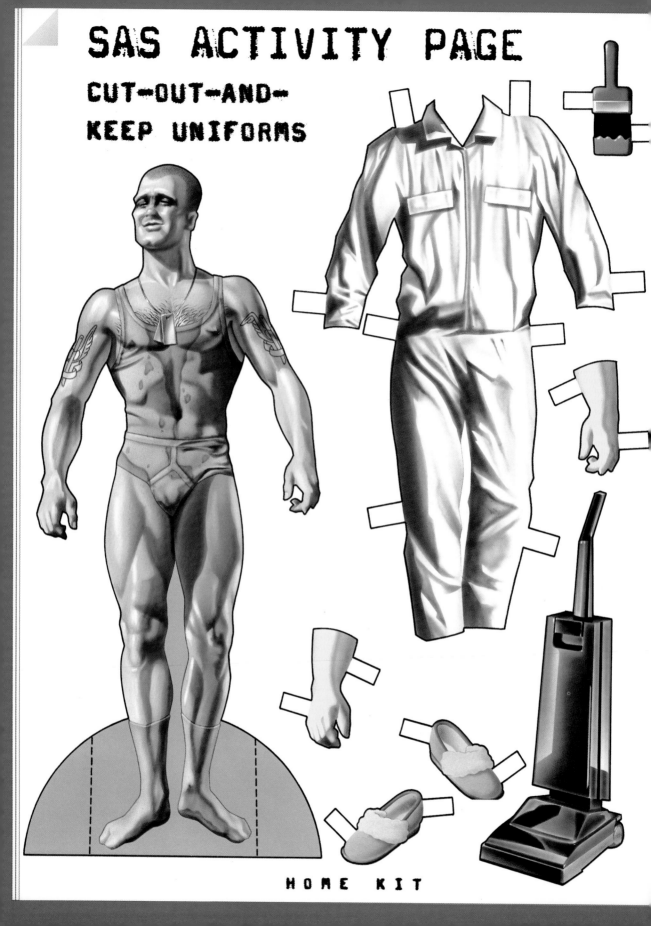

DRESS KIT

*I've been cold before, but never that cold. Bitter, bitter cold. Chill the bone cold. And then some. The whole team was holed up in the most god-awful LUP you could imagine. A small cesspit with a totalled Renault providing minimal cover. Two hundred yards to our right was a three-star Michelin restaurant with a sign which, Side Salad told me said 'Rooms Available'. To our left, shimmering in the distance, the lights of St Malo. In front, France. Behind us, Mother Channel.*

After all we've been through it was amazing we're all still together, but we were – me, Side Salad, Rupert, Mousse, Scud, Fiji Bob and 13 mad cows. It reminded me of Hereford.

'Would they fuck us?' The French, not the cows, that is. It was a nasty question but one that had to be addressed. The French eat garlic, wear berets and play *pétanque*, but these are national characteristics for which they can't be blamed, and it didn't necessarily follow that they were all shit-stabbers.

I had decided that as soon as it got dark we would tab forty klicks southeast, trek back ten klicks northwest, dogleg thirty klicks east-north east and then full steam ahead for the final ten klicks. If we got separated we would rendezvous in the Pudding Shop, Istanbul, a really friendly restaurant which allows back-packers to put up messages for their mates. No problem. If it wasn't for the fucking mental cows.

'Never work with animals,' my old man, who used to be a circus ringmaster, was forever telling me. Very true, old man. Ever since the Chinook dropped us and two dozen cattle into a point

nearly a hundred metres to the north of here, the cows have been nothing but trouble. An undisciplined rabble at the start, they are now disintegrating. And the last three days have convinced me that hell is not other people, but other cows.

Yet it had all seemed so different when we were formally introduced to them back at Brize Norton. It was one of those wonderful June days that linger in the memory: clear blue sky, slightest of breezes, the cows contentedly chewing their cud. Our mission seemed simplicity itself. Buzz over to enemy territory, cows and men parachute down to DOP, march with cows to designated farm, infiltrate cows into foreign herd, buzz back. Simple it may have been, but I still explained it very slowly. It is regimental policy to explain orders as if nobody's got a clue what's going on – and this rule applies with bells on when there are cows in the team.

Everything went smoothly until the drop. Fuck did those cows hit the ground at speed. With hindsight, I can now see that the standard-issue army 'chutes were not designed with half-a-ton of cow in mind. But if we all possessed hindsight there would only be heroes in this game. Suffice it to say, we left a lot of dead meat five klicks west of St Malo. There was no time for remorse; the cows knew the score when they joined the Regiment. And if you worried about cows getting hurt and killed you'd be on antidepressants for the rest of your life.

Anyhow, we had problems enough with the cows that hadn't kicked the bucket. Sensing they would be the weakest in the group, I placed them second in the line and we started to tab across Northern France. Not for long. Every ten paces or so one of the clapped-out old milkers would stagger around and then collapse in a heap. For a while we simply put them back on their feet and tried to continue the tab. Progress was cruelly slow. Before we had gone a hundred yards the cows and the men were sweating like rapists.

Realising the seriousness of the situation I called the men together for a kefuffle and started by stating the obvious, 'We're not going very fast.' There was a murmur of agreement, followed by silence. A silence broken, eventually, by a muted moo and the sound of another cow crashing to the ground. That was too much for Fiji Bob. He nabbed over to the cow, hauled it on to his shoulders and yomped over the horizon. Scud, not to be outdone, was the next to have a crack. He half-lifted the cow, groaned and collapsed in a heap underneath it. As daylight was approaching we had no option but to scuttle back behind the stalled Renault and leave Scud in a hugely compromised position.

Last night we finally extricated him. He had lost any feeling in his legs and his voice was squeaky but he was in better shape than the cow. In a last-ditch effort to shake off hunger, Scud had taken huge chunks out of the wretched beast's midriff. Let's hope, for Scud's sake anyway, that those anti-CJD injections are what they are cracked up to be.

Spirits sagged. Side Salad, in particular, was finding it hard to cope with being in the company of all that Aberdeen Angus and not able to eat it. He kept murmuring 'Carpaccio, grated parmesan, dash of rosemary' like a mantra. Rupert, meanwhile, kept telling us a really boring anecdote which ended with him snogging his French exchange. And Scud, well, Scud was having problems balancing.

Ten minutes before daybreak, Fiji Bob returned. Cowless. I immediately court-martialled him. He may not be too clever at the language but he knows the rules. You don't just disappear over the horizon leaving your mates in the shit. It was a close-run thing but the block vote of the cows swung it against him. He shrugged at the verdict, picked up another cow, and disappeared over the horizon. That man is history vis à vis the Regiment.

Sometimes a leader has to make a decision. Decision-making defines leadership. And at 14.05 on a grey afternoon one klick west of St Malo I made one. I tabbed into St Malo, made a reverse-charge call to my wife and got her to book us five ferry tickets to England via St Hellier.

The cows. The cows we left behind. Sometimes you have to make sacrifices in this game.

# PAM

REGIMENTAL PIN-UP

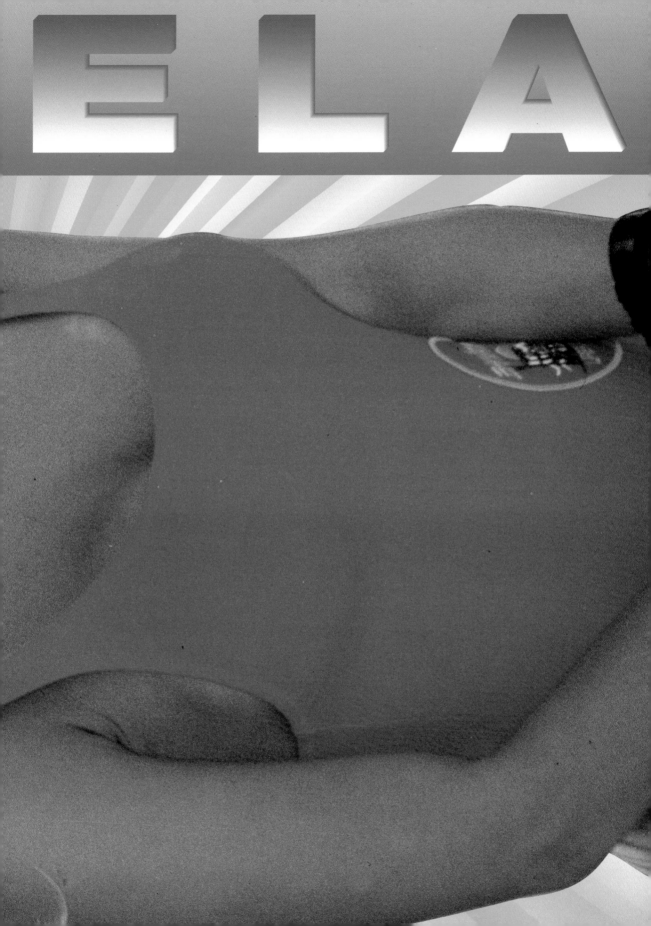

## X SQUADRON

# Vietnam — Heart of Darkness

X Squadron's contribution to covert warfare against the Viet Cong was stupendous. But it was their search and destroy mission to the Philippines that distinguished them on this occasion. Word came in from American Intelligence that one of their own men had gone native up river. His megalomania and dark philosophy had left many people dead or worse. The man was out of control and pretty soon the Squadron were drifting slowly up river to the heart of darkness — weapons cocked, searching for the glint of metal or the sound of clapper on wood.

After two weeks they found his spoor. A polystyrene coffee cup and a clapperboard. Shortly afterwards they came upon him, directing a drug-induced battle scene with a fleet of commandeered helicopters. They bore down on him as he shovelled pasta into his gaping mouth whilst screaming, 'Make it sexy. I want these choppers to look horny as hell. Sweep those extras bodies out of the way. They knew the risk when they agreed to the napalming.' This man had to be stopped. Who knew what further havoc he would wreak if allowed to extend shooting by another month? The Squadron CO took charge of the set and closed down the production. Francis Ford Coppola was later put before a War Crimes Tribunal and found guilty of *Finian's Rachbow*.

ABOVE: TORTURED BY TOMMY STEELE
BELOW: COPPOLA — OUT OF CONTROL

# SAS CODES OF CONDUCT

Over the last few years there has been a lot of controversy about the way the SAS goes about its business. Therefore we are very happy to announce that we are actively trying to obtain a Citizens Charter Mark for the Regiment so that the public may be certain of Hereford's status as a centre of excellence for devastating termination of manpower and a responsible state-sponsored mayhem service provider.

The new updated rules of engagement are very simple. If you are not threatened in any way by the target, do not engage. If they make for their weapon or show any signs of being the *Guardian's* foreign correspondent, let them have it.

**Hostile posture. Slot him.**

**COMBAT**

# COMBAT POSITIONS

RIGHT

**GOOD CHARGE**

WRONG

**BAD CHARGE**

**GOOD COVERING POSITION**

**BAD COVERING POSITION**

**GOOD SPACING**

**BAD SPACING**

# PRACTICAL

At heart we are all schoolboys, aren't we? And like any self-respecting schoolboy we need to let off steam occasionally. What better way to achieve this than cracking a practical joke? Good for morale and good for a laugh. Of course, being in the Regiment, when we do a practical joke we do it properly. In the SAS jokes are no laughing matter. We take them seriously. As an indication of the way we go about having a laugh, I have compiled a list of the top five jokes played during my time in the Regiment.

## WALES 1982

You can lose your sense of humour during training and, I have to admit, I almost lost mine after this superb practical joke. We'd been stranded in the Brecon Beacons for a week and a half without a hexy and people were seriously getting on each other's tits. Nothing wrong with that; it's when people are being nice you've got to be careful.

Then, Side Salad said to me, 'Hey, No Mates, have I ever told you that I think you're a great bloke?' 'No,' I replied truthfully. 'You couldn't just run over behind that bush and get me a sprig of rosemary?' It seemed the least I could do. How was I to know they'd rigged the bush up with C4 and HE and that when I reached the bush both me and it were blown all the way to Powys? Fair one.

## A SOUTH AMERICAN COUNTRY 1985

Me and a bunch of lads were sent over to the other side of the world to help the drugs trade run more smoothly. Basically there were too many middlemen wanting a cut and it was our job to downsize the operation and guarantee greater returns. As you can imagine, by simply doing our job we made quite a few enemies. Take away someone's livelihood and they aren't going to thank you. Making a swift exit can be fairly crucial; therefore I wasn't hugely amused to discover, when the order came through to make ours, that I had been locked in my hotel room. It took the Head Shed six months to negotiate my eventual release, during which time I had some very nasty moments but, on the plus side, learned Spanish. Fair One.

## HEREFORD-CHRISTMAS PARTY 1987

Let's face it, I was well bladdered. Kimberley III was gobbing off at home, my promotion to joke-corporal looked as if it might never come through and I had an upset stomach. So I was really giving it some cider-lager mix. Well gone. When Mousse says to me, 'Hey, No Mates, I reckon that boiler at the bar really fancies you.' Now, even in my reduced state I could tell she wasn't much of a looker, but sometimes a man's got

# JOKES

to be a man. I put on the old charm and before you knew it 'Night Boat to Cairo' was on the juke box and my hands were all over her big, fat, sexy arse and I was murmuring sweet nothings in her ear. Bit of a shock, then, when her wig fell off and I saw I was in a clinch with Scud. Took some living down, I can tell you. Fair one.

## THE KILLING HOUSE 1989

We were killing time in the Killing House when I found myself the butt of this blinding practical joke. I'd being going on for some time about the need to make our training a bit more realistic, so when on the last day of term the lads suggested I be Terry Waite, I was all for it. They promptly trussed me up against the radiator, turned it on full blast, turned the lights off and fucked off for their Christmas holidays. Initially, I failed to see the funny side. Well, I'm only human, aren't I? But by the time they returned three weeks later there was a grin on my face. Fair one.

## MALAYSIA 1991

The oldest joke in the book, and Muggins here had to fall for it. Probably because I had my head well stuck into a book about English feudal history, I didn't realise that Fiji Bob, or some other joker, had burnt a hole the size of a football into my 'chute while we were waiting to make our drop. Off I jumped, pulled the cord – no deceleration. Only a fool wouldn't have been frightened, but I could see the funny side when I landed in an immense dung-heap. Sure, only a foot to my left was a dangerous-looking spike which would have creamed me – but live fast, die young. Fair one.

NB Reading through the list I notice that every single one of these pranks was directed at me. The odds against such a coincidence are similar to getting five numbers and the bonus ball in a rollover week.

# THE SAS GUIDE TO THE
# Family

## CAMPING

A great way to take some time off and hone your skills. The secret of a successful camping holiday is planning. Never forget that a minor detail missed equals fuck-up guaranteed. A maxim illustrated by the time when I took the family for a ten-day winter break to the middle of Dartmoor, and owing to pressure of space failed to pack any baby food.

Due to this oversight the twins returned to civilisation painfully thin and had to spend Christmas on an intravenous drip at the local hospital. And I was forced to undergo some tricky questioning from the Social Services. It goes without saying that they got nothing out of me other than the Big Four – number, rank, name, date of birth.

*Paradise*

## TREKKING

Another favourite with the lads – we like our busman's holidays in the SAS. The vital thing here is distribution. Each Bergen must be evenly packed with provisions so that if, for whatever reason, you lose a member of the family, the rest of the troop can successfully complete the trek. Good tactics and good for morale, as I have discovered that people, whether they are seventeen stone or twelve pounds and six ounces, want and expect equal loads. You should see how the twins squeal if I don't fill their Bergens with the full 209 pounds.

## THORPE PARK

You are never going to get your money's worth at any theme park unless you get your priorities in order. What do we want out of this expedition? What are we prepared to forego if time gets tight? Is it worth taking advantage of the three-rides-for-the-price-of-two Big Dipper offer?

The easiest way to screw up the entire operation is for a member of the family to bollocks the precision timing by wasting half an hour in the queue for the public toilets. To avoid this I always elect my wife to carry a one gallon plastic container for use as a piss can on our visits to Thorpe Park.

## CARAVANNING

A great way of saving money on exorbitant hotel bills and a chance for the family to spend a fortnight in a confined space and really get to know each other. When space is limited, leadership is vital, so I appoint myself platoon leader with the experienced Kimberley as my 2 i/c.

The thing to worry about here is people being nice to each other. There is nothing that undermines a family unit quicker than members of that unit complimenting each other. I, therefore, concentrate most of my energies on keeping up a steady stream of abuse for the two weeks while we are holed up in the 'van.

# Holiday

## SPAIN

One of the few European hot spots which actually welcomes the British soldier, and very convenient for Gibraltar. This comes in handy if you feel like escaping from the family and spending some quality time with a bunch of squaddies pulling babes and talking war.

When AWOL from the family the brief is simple – get in there, do the business, and then come back. And the emphasis is on the 'coming back'. Over the past decade, the Regiment has sustained an unhealthy level of casualties from good men being taken captive by cheap Spanish tarts, never to return. *Caveat Emptor*.

*We will remember him*

**Rest and Recreation**

**Board games are a good way of killing time during slack moments. But amongst highly trained men, it is best not to let minor incidents turn into major confrontations.**

**Andy's tip: 'Never, ever cheat at Hungry Hippo'.**

ANDY'S LEISURE TIPS

## 'If they'd built the bloody bypass we wouldn't be in this bloody hole.'

*W*e were yomping through Reading in textbook style. Mousse was scout, making sure we moved on the compass bearing and using the nightsight to ensure we weren't going to walk into anything nasty. Second in line was Rupert, who still hadn't shrugged off a polo injury and was starting to hallucinate. Then me, Side Salad, Scud and Fiji Bob.

Reading city centre is a bastard at the best of times. On a cold March night, it's the worst place on earth. We had already had a contact outside the Student Union bar, which so nearly developed into a fire-fight, and I was desperate to get in touch with the Head Shed to inform them of our predicament. Above me I heard a BA plane winging its way to Heathrow. I placed a hand on Rupert's shoulder and said, 'We're going to stop and try and make TACBE.' Side Salad whipped out his Magellan and I whispered, 'This is Bravo Six Six Six, we're outside Do It All in central Reading and we're in the shit.' Nothing.

A car alarm went off and all was confusion. When everything subsided I turned into the wind to tell Mousse and Rupert the score. 'For fuck's sake,' I whispered, 'where's everyone else gone?' Let's get one thing straight – no blame can be attached to me. Why did Rupert just press on? What was Mousse doing charging ahead? Why didn't Fiji Bob sneak round the back and rein them in? Johnny Fiji may be an adequate fighter but he can be very dense.

Enough analysis – the upshot was that we'd be taking on the tree-huggers with a reduced force. We spent the next day holed up in a café on the outskirts of Reading, clinging to the radiators to stay warm and hoping that Mousse and Rupert might drop in for a milky cappuccino. No one spoke much. We all knew that within 24 hours we would be on the receiving end of everything that Johnny Tree-hugger could throw at us. A sobering thought. Our mission: to slot tree-huggers and take out trees, with extreme prejudice. Tough call.

However much you plan, however much you train, however much you think, there's no legislating for fate. And fate was in an ugly mood that March morning. First Side Salad unused to greasy food, succumbed to a chronic bout of food poisoning. There was nothing for it but to leave him in a public toilet deep in enemy territory. Second, I slipped and sprained my ankle. None of the 'It's O.K' bollocks from me, because if you try to play the he-man you can endanger the whole patrol. I told Scud and Fiji Bob about my ankle; they laughed and went on without me. Fair game. No one said the job would be easy.

Alone, I held out for longer than was humanly possible. Five minutes later inevitably I was captured. I like to think that despite my sore ankle I took out a few trees before they got me.

I gave them nothing. Just the Big Four of number, rank, name and date of birth which was all the tree-huggers were allowed to ask for under the Geneva Convention. Then the hippies brought their fucking guitars out and I moved on to my cover story. We were all working as researchers for a Channel 4 series called *An A–Z of Trees*. It was a weak story. I knew nothing about television, but it might buy me precious time. To give it credibility I pointed out of the window at an oak and said, 'Nice tree'. One of the tree-huggers grunted and I took advantage of this show of friendship to ask him for a brew. 'Make it yourself,' he said.

Alone in my tree hut I thought about the others. Had Side Salad gone down in the public toilet? Was Rupert's polo injury playing up? But mainly I thought about escape. Of course, there was no possibility of escape with one, often two, tree-huggers smoking spliffs twenty yards below me. It's not like the movies, you know.

I awoke covered in shit – Scud's shit. Having been deprived of human contact for so long I almost welcomed it. Scud had an amazing tale to tell. He had taken out a dozen tree-huggers, many more trees and was carefully dismantling a tree hut when he spotted a stray long-hair running for cover. Instinctively he had launched one of his trademark flying head-butts, only for his timing to go awry and have his forehead miss the fuzzy and hit a boulder. Taking advantage of his considerable headache, the tree-huggers had rounded him up. Unlucky.

We have been cooped up here nearly 24 hours now. Doesn't anyone know we are here? Doesn't anyone care? I've just experienced the lowest point of my life. Concorde flew over and I found myself shouting, 'Do it! Fucking bomb me! I'm down here!'

Did they take any notice? Did they, fuck?

But I pulled through, fought back, struggled to

swallow down my disappointment. You have to be tough in this game. Really tough, because minutes later one of the long-hairs took advantage of Scud's sleeping to invite me down to listen to him play guitar. I blocked my ears without using my hands (just one of the special skills you learn on training). Then he offered me one of those funny rolled-up cigarettes that smell of danger. No way, José. You'll never catch a member of the Regiment inhaling a prohibited substance. I pretended to smoke it, of course, purely to try and sneak a look at his watch. If you lose track of the minutes, then you'll lose track of the hours, then the days, and before you know it you don't know what year you're in. He wasn't wearing a watch so this ploy failed, but the important thing is that I didn't inhale.

**Tree camo. Tried and tested throughout the British Army since Burnham Wood moved to Dunstinane.**

After he had finished his smoke he wanted to talk politics. I explained that I was just a TV researcher who had been sent out to do a researcher's job. I had no interest in the war. I was just doing Thatcher and Major's dirty work while they sat at home watching Sharpe and drinking gin and tonic. Personally, I had no beef with the long hairs. It's a free planet, man. He told me to chill and rolled another spliff.

I really thought I was about to get through when suddenly I came over all paranoid. This happen when you've been taken captive for a long time according to Terry Waite's book. One minute we were talking trees and the next I was convinced tha the long hair fancied Scud, Scud preferred the long hair and neither of them cared for me. Then the trees started to take the piss out of me. I was woke by Scud. I was sweating like a rapist but otherwise i pretty good order. We tabbed to Reading and hitched up the M4 towards Hereford.

Gilbert

## THE FIJIAN ZODIAC

### Fiji Bob's STARS

## GeorgeBushalam

### MAY 20–JUNE 20

GEORGEBUSHALAMS are a proud, confident, assertive star sign with the ability to make quick decisions and act rationally. No, only joking. Generally they are sad old has-beens, famous for not being Ronald Reagan. GEORGEBUSHALAMS enjoy prevarication, fudging and lipreading.

### THIS WEEK

Uranus in conjunction with an old joke will see you ignored by world leaders on Monday. On Tuesday your 'phone will fail to ring. On Wednesday you will offer to open a supermarket in Little Bigot, Idaho. On Thursday the mayor of Little Bigot will ring to tell you not to bother as they have now had an offer from Ronald McDonald. On Friday Readers Digest will inform you by post that you have not been selected for entry in their prize draw.

Lucky sandwich: Oliver North in a sesame seed bap
Lucky after shave: 'Scent of a Woman' by Thatcher

## THE FIJIAN ZODIAC

# MEMORANDUM

From:   Head Shed — General Sir Peter De La Billionère

To:     Small Outhouse — Corporal Rory McDade

Re:     Embassy Siege Enquiry

Divisional HQ and Battalion Command have finally handed down their verdict on the Iranian Embassy Siege débâcle. I quote from the report of their enquiry which ran for two volumes plus appendices.

"Due to a navigational error, X squadron failed to support Red Team by attacking the rear of the Iranian Embassy as ordered. Instead they inadvertently stormed the London Borough of Kensington's Planning Department. Hundreds of applications for extensions and conservatories were destroyed in the ensuing bloodbath. The Regiment apologises to the families of those who were the victims of this operational mistake and accept that Corporal McDade's offer to 'tidy up' was not acceptable compensation for the incident. We have hereby decided that the squadron in question should have their commissary privileges withdrawn."

I begged and pleaded with them, Rory. I pointed out all our previous successes, even allowing them access to the squadron's regimental history, but this simply seemed to stiffen their resolve. As of 1300 hours today, X squadron will no longer be allowed to eat with the rest of the Regiment.

I have, of course, wrung certain concessions from them over this matter and you will all be pleased to learn that they have designated the Hereford Happy Eater as a suitable alternative. On a more personal note, I have recommended you for the DSM for the most civil servants destroyed in a single action.

# THE LOADED BERGEN

# PUZZLE PAGE

## SPOT THE DIFFERENCE

**SAS SOLDIER**

**IRA GUNMAN**

A highly trained SAS soldier has to be able to recognise the enemy in a combat situation. That is why the regiment provided this handy identification guide.

# SAS FIELDCRAFT

## BY GENERAL SIR PETER DE LA BILLIONÈRE

THE SPOOKS of Le Carré have their 'spycraft' – those little tips and tricks that help turn them from Oxbridge pederasts into Oxbridge pederasts with diplomatic immunity. We in the SAS have our own little secrets – things that have kept my lads on their toes and out of trouble around the world.

## LUP

The LUP or 'Legs Up Position' is a vital tool of concealment. Invented by X Squadron founder Colonel Worsnip, it is based on a unique theory:

*'The last thing the enemy expects to see in the majestic desert landscape is a pair of army boots sticking straight up in the air. The sight is so incongruous that the enemy's brain simply blocks it out, thus rendering the troop invisible.'* COLONEL WORSNIP

Colonel Worsnip walked with a pronounced limp until his death after being strafed from the knee down by Rommel's Afrika Korps.

## SEXUAL DISTRACTION

The enemy have been known to use sex as a very effective weapon and many's the time a well-equipped trooper has been rendered incapable by a strategically placed female, not to mention a camel in a tutu on one occasion which we won't talk about until after the court martial.

*Sexual deviancy of any kind is absolutely prohibited on the field. What you do with a goat, a tub of axle grease and a bicycle pump in the privacy of your own greenhouse is your own affair, but there'll be no perversion on duty. We're not the Household Cavalry.*

## EDUCATION

It's also important for all soldiers to be absolutely up to speed with the world situation.

*Spare time should usefully be spent absorbing current affairs.*

## BE PREPARED

The most important element of fieldcraft is preparation. Preparation, preparation, preparation. Preparation H is very effective for the older officer. All those years squatting on sand dunes tend to take their toll.

*Corporal McGrabb in Bosnia discovering that bad preparation has left him with nowhere to plug in the microwave.*

## EQUIPMENT

It is no use dragging along the finest and shiniest war machinery the taxpayer can afford, if no one knows how to operate it. Losing the manual for the laser-guided howitzer can result in you using it the wrong way round and decimating your own regiment.

*Take-off and landing are tricky manoeuvres to master in a Chinook. In this case the part of the manual dealing with landing was used as toilet paper by one unthinking co-pilot.*

*Playing badminton with the heads of enemy casualties is bad manners and frankly unhygienic.*

## BATTLE ETIQUETTE

We all remember the First World War story of the Christmas truce when German and British troops exchanged pleasantries and played one-thousand-and-five-a-side football at the Somme. Well, today there are also certain things which are simply not done.

## PHOTOGENIC STRATEGY

The first casualty of war is Ruth, but she knew the risks when she joined the nursing corps. The second is getting the war photographers to get your good side. We spent bally ages trying to get the make-up right on that Falklands picture with the raised Union Jack. Posing effectively could not be more important. Below is a perfect example.

*Pointing off into the middle distance and looking noble is a prerequisite.*

# 55TH ANNUAL SAS REUNION PARTY

## AT THE — BALLROOM IN — AT —

*Those wishing to know the date of the above event should go to the third cubicle on the left in the lavatory of Waterloo Station where they will receive sealed orders. Fly to Bremen, get a taxi to Le Havre and tab across to Bilbao after destroying your ID cards and burying your dog tags. After arriving in Burkina Faso, go directly to the Ouagodougou Hilton and check in to room 311. Abseil out of the window at 1700 hours and crawl across the car park to the blue Mondeo. Get in and drive to Cape Town. Take an unscheduled flight to Algeria and sign up with the Foriegn Legion under the name of John Smith to avoid suspicion. Escape at 1300 hours by hailing the 322 bus from Algiers and asking the driver to let you off at Karachi. Open your sealed orders and make your own way back to the Hereford Harvester Inn. Latecomers will be shot in the legs.*

### GUEST SPEAKER:
Fred Bloggs

### MASTER OF CEREMONIES:
Fred Bloggs

### CABARET:
Fred Bloggs and his amazing talking Bergen.

❖

The Flying Privates featuring Fred Bloggs

❖

and Little Fred Bloggs the quirky comic –
*'A smile, a song and a full magazine of tracer'*

❖

### CARRIAGES AT 11.00
### TANKS AT 12.30
### BOGIES AT FOUR O'CLOCK

# FIRST COURSE

*Seven chicken pick'em ups with argie sauce*
*Beef Basra flambee done to a turn*

⚜

# SECOND COURSE

S A S   H A P P Y   M E A L

*Big McGrabb and fries with choice of soft drink and a toy*
*(Beretta pistol with novelty hand grip)*

*Twelve sachets of brown dehydrated stew,*
*a jug of pond water and a hexy block*

⚜

# DESSERT

*Rice pudding*
*Hexy block smeared with a choice of jams*

⚜

ANDY McGRABB'S MAP WHICH HE SMUGGLED
OUT OF LONDON AND HAD SIGNED BY ALL
HIS PALS.

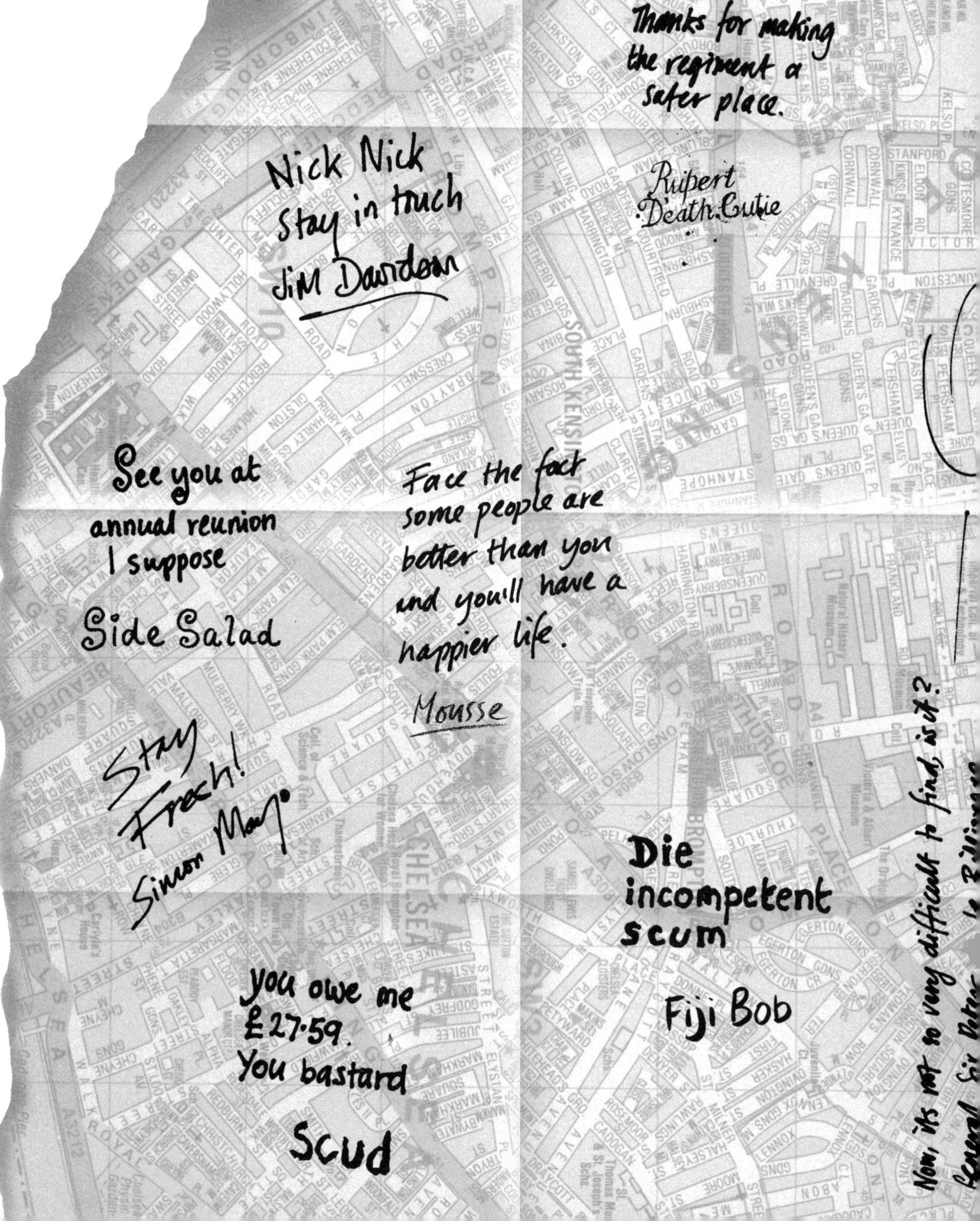

Thanks for making
the regiment a
safer place.

Rupert
Death Cutie

Nick Nick
Stay in touch
Jim Davidson

See you at
annual reunion
I suppose

Side Salad

Face the fact
some people are
better than you
and you'll have a
happier life.

Mousse

Stay
Fresh!
Simon May

Die
incompetent
scum

Fiji Bob

You owe me
£27.59.
You bastard

Scud

Now, it's not so very difficult to find, is it?

General Sir Peter la B'Wimmin

# MEMORANDUM

From: Head Shed — General Sir Peter De La Billionère

To: Small Outhouse — Corporal Andy McGrabb

Re: Disbandment of the Squadron

I don't mind telling you there's a lump in my throat as I type these words.

~~AFTER THE BUSINESS~~ After the business we don't talk about, Divisional HQ have told me that they have no alternative but to disband the Squadron for good. Frankly, I am utterly appalled at this brazen act of treachery and, whilst one doesn't want to seem vindictive, I feel the whole damn lot of them should be shot for treason. If they hadn't taken away our weapons, uniforms and underwear, I'd be tempted to carry out the sentence myself. Their feeble excuse for disbanding us is included in this memo I received today from Personnel:

'Due to the extraordinary lack of operational success in X Squadron's entire 55 years and the disablement of its one competent soldier, the Regiment has decided that the other members of the troop would be better employed somewhere where their unique talents can be better utilised. Such as the Navy or the RAF, or the programme-scheduling department of a major broadcaster. An outplacement counsellor has been appointed. Please leave the barracks as you would wish to find them and lock all unused stationery in the bottom drawer of your desk, first removing the 75 copies of *Boy Bikers* magazine and the baby oil dispenser.'

Heartless bastards. I have left a set of claymore mines in the out-tray and booby-trapped the drinks cabinet. My last orders are that the men leave by tank through the Personnel Department. Please remember to put the cat out.

~~GOODBYE~~ Goodbye, my brave boys. If any of you need a leg up in civvy street just drop me a line at: Mighty Morphin Power Squirrels Quality Control Dept, Taiwan Toy Company, Ninja Badger Buildings, Basingstoke.

# Fiji Bob speaks

I WOULD BE the first to admit that I'm not a great talker. In fact, 99 times out of 100 I would prefer not to say anything at all. As Uncle Tuingamalla says 'A loud bell makes the most noise'. I guess I just come from a family of quiet bells.

Instead of talking I like to fade into the background and listen – which is just as well, because in X Squadron there's always so much to listen to. Andy, Scud, Mousse, even Side Salad, pour out words out of their mouths like Gwaa, the Volcano God, sucks lather out of the great heaving bosom of Mother Earth. Few of them make sense but that doesn't seem to matter. The important thing is to talk and the less you actually have to say the more words you take to say it. It's very strange. Their legs seem to get tired well before their tongues.

'As Andy always says "Each to their own abilities". I guess mine is freight.'

I never thought it would be like this when, back home in Fiji, Uncle Tuingamalla took me out shark-wrestling one day and told me all about the SAS. The way he described this tribe of black-clad, highly secretive warriors was noble, heroic, thrilling. They kept themselves to themselves; their daring deeds as invisible to the world's gloating gaze as a lesser-spotted jam-jaalam on a paw paw tree. When called upon, they would leap from the lair and strike like a sea python on the enemies of truth and justice. As soon as the job was done they would fade away into the night, like the guiding spirits that lead fish-ermen to their grounds. They never boasted of what hey had done or courted publicity. Their only hanks was the knowledge inside that they had once again dared and won.

This was the Regiment I thought I was joining all those years ago when I packed a few sandwiches and a banana tree into a trunk, said goodbye to Mum, Dad and my 17 brothers and started to swim for Hereford. That things turned out differently is, as I have now realised, only to be expected. After all, as the old Fijian poem puts it:

*The wise turtle*
*Swims for the shore*
*Knowing all too well*
*The sand is made of sea.*

Despite our many difficulties, no one was more sad than I when I heard that the General had finally decided to disband the Squadron. Of course I understood his reasons. I even agreed with some of them. Things had changed. People had moved on like the east breeze across the ocean. There was only so much I could do with one finger, two toes and a battery-powered wheelchair.

But that didn't mean I wanted it all to end, just like that, with a single memo pinned to the announcements board in the local library and a quick farewell meal at the Pizza Hut in the High Street. Somehow I expected more of the fam-ily to which I had given my life for the past six years – along with three limbs, an eye and several quite important internal organs.

Still, I suppose the last 10 years have not been entirely wasted. I have travelled the world, met and killed many interesting people and learnt many vital military skills, like desktop publish-ing, exploiting secondary rights and finding the best production company for your TV tie-in.

More than this I have been part of a team. Andy, Scud, Mousse, Side Salad, Rupert. There are many things I could say about them, so many in fact that I could probably write a book, if only the lawyers would let me and Andy hadn't forged my signature on that contract his publisher sent round before I got my own agent.

Perhaps it's for the best. As Uncle Tuingamalla says 'The shortest man tells the tallest tale' and I could never hope to be as short as Andy, however hard I tried. Besides, when all is said and done and the Sun has gone off to pay courtship to the Moon, there is nothing to say. We went in, I did what we had to do, we came back and put the kettle on. Simple. The rest is just words on a page. As the old Fijian poem puts it:

*I showed you a rock*
*And you claimed to see mountains*
*I showed you a dog*
*And you claimed to see dragons*
*I showed you my heart*
*And you claimed to see nothing.*
*Perhaps you need your eyes tested.*

## Andy McGrabb

Naturally it took me a bit of time to adjust to life in the TA. For a start, only having to turn up for one weekend a month meant that although I was doing more work than I had in the Regiment, I was receiving considerably less money. This didn't go down too well with Kimberley IV and no one was at all surprised, least of all me, when I returned from a particularly punishing weekend to discover that Kimberley IV had done a runner. Fair one. In my experience of Kimberleys there's normally another one lurking behind the next corner.

The biggest shock about living on civvy street has been how rarely you see your old mates. You read a lot of sentimental gumph about ex-members of the Regiment meeting for a few beers and a chin-wag about the old times. Nonsense, I haven't seen any of them.

## Scud

When International Tobacco offered me a job selling fags to the Africans I jumped at it quicker than I can smoke a Rothmans. My first posting was Burundi. Fair one. I'd like to think that despite a political situation that can only be described as volatile, I did my bit to help International Tobacco penetrate this tricky part of the globe. Certainly, they seemed to think so, because within three months my brief was extended to cover the whole of Central Africa. A tough beat, but not insuperable. I would have to say that you meet a nicer type of person in this branch of the tobacco industry than you did in the Regiment. And I would like to thank everyone at Comic Relief for all their support.

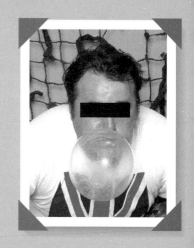

## Rupert

In many ways a prep school isn't so dissimilar to the Regiment. A group of chaps pulling together towards the same end. Except here at Hewitts we are all struggling to pass Common Entrance rather than promote World Peace. No matter; discipline and leadership are still important. A tidy uniform indicates a tidy mind. It was ever thus.

Teaching PE has been a challenge, but a hugely enjoyable one. Supervising boys shinning up ropes, attempting the high bar for the first time and washing themselves down in the showers. In a very real sense it has turned out to be more of a hobby than a job.

### Mousse McCracken

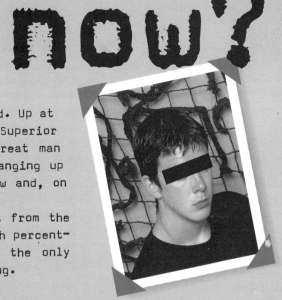

No one told me hairdressing would be this hard. Up at seven every morning and down to Giannini's Superior Hair Care to clean the floors before the great man makes his entrance. Then my day is filled hanging up people's jackets, making our customers a brew and, on a good day, washing their hair.

In many ways the salon isn't so different from the mess at Hereford. Similar magazines and a high percentage of people who know their hair. Perhaps the only thing I miss is the excellent air-conditioning.

### Side Salad

Before you ask, no, I didn't expect to land my own prime-time TV show within three weeks of leaving the Regiment. But then you make your own luck, especially in catering.

It just so happened that my brand of cooking, barbecuing under pressure, was exactly what the BBC were looking for, so when they heard I was available they moved fast. That's show business. It's nice to be recognised on the streets; it's less nice having to make the statutory 'It's in every cook's contract' appearance on *Ready Steady Cook*.

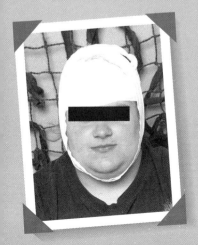

### Fiji Bob

Having never taken a holiday while I was with the Regiment, I thought a few days in Liechtenstein would do me some good. Yet, and life can be like that, it proved to be the start of my problems. Feeling ever so slightly refreshed, and even more bored, after my sojourn in Liechtenstein, I immediately ran into problems at customs. They marked me down as an asylum seeker and before I knew it I was held hostage in a hangar towards the east end of Gatwick Village.

It didn't take me long to extricate myself from that particular predicament, but it has taken me longer to get over the insult. To say I held the Regiment together for over a decade would be to understate my contribution, yet when I return from holiday I am treated in this shabby manner. Revenge is the only answer.

# GLOSSARY

**AWACS** Large spy plane full of smug, crew-cut Americans

**Bergen** Gloomy Swedish flim director. Also large heavy rucksack for carrying half a house (see Tab)

**Bone** Top-secret tactical weapon used against guard dogs

**Brew** The art of making yourself a cup of tea without putting down your weapon and/or spilling it all down your new balaclava

**Bulk Up** Large meal eaten before going on a mission or, if your name is Fiji Bob, after every third breath or so

**CO** Commanding Officer. Also, more usually, an official title added to a squadron's name when it's being prepared for flotation on the stock market

**Claymore** Thin earthenware pipe, much favoured by crofters in the Outer Hebrides

**Coms** Pinkoes, lefties, CND bearded bastards - shoot the lot of them on sight, I say

**COP** Coming Out Party. Not that I have ever been to one, you understand

**Cuds** Countryside. Also polite swear word as in 'Oi you Fergie. What the cudding hell do you think you're doing, trying to charge us for protecting you?'

**Dinkie** Penis, well that's what my scoutmaster used to call it anyway

**DOP** Drop Off Point. Mine is usually about 1.30 except if there's a sex chat on the telly

**E&E** Eric & Ernie i.e. a couple of bloody comedians. Also Escape & Evasion

**ERV** Emergency Rendevous i.e. in the car park behind Superdrug if her old man's come home early

**ET** Doe-eyed Alien who fell over a lot and said Ouch

**FOB** Foreign Office Balls-up i.e. anything that's happened before we have to go in

**FRV** Frightened Reckless Virgins. Name of pub band that plays in the Lamb & Bucket, Hereford

**GPMG** General Purpose Machine Gun or 'Giant Paddies May carry Guns.' Standard warning to troops in Ireland.

**Green Slime** Special hair preparation used by Mousse McKracken when he's got split ends. Also intelligence officers, laughably

**Hard Routine** If wandering around in the freezing cold with all your gear on eating cold food and plants is your idea of fun well it's not mine. For fanatics and weirdos only

**HE** Low-impact naturists porn mag. Very usual if you're going to Islamic countries or working closely with cabinet ministers

**Head Shed** Headquarters. Why they can't get themselves housed in a proper building after all these years is quite beyond me

**Hexy** Small block of fast-burning fuel. Also useful for handing out as sweets to gullible native children. Oh how we laughed...

**Infil/Exfil** Infiltration and Exfiltration. Personally I was crap at chemistry at school

**LUP** Legs Up Position

**Magellan** Some sort of flashy electronic navigation aid. Personally I don't see what's wrong with using the compass in the heel of my Clarke's Attackers

**MSR** Main Supply Route i.e. any road that leads to your nearest Tesco

**NBC** American TV network that specialises in turning the Olympic Games into a girly soap-opera

**Net** Technical term for small circular mesh attached to a length of bamboo and used to catch tadpoles

**NVA** Night Vision Aid i.e. a pound of carrots or Donald Duck pencil torch

**NVG** Fast French train running between Paris and Lyon. Gets packed at the weekend and in the holidays, so book early if you want a window seat

**OP** Something old people seem to have when they go into hospitals

**OPEC** Some kind of international organisation that sets oil prices

**PE** Intense physical activity

**Pear-shaped** Something that's shaped like a pear i.e... pears

**PLC** What every squadron should look to becoming if the books sell and you're looking to re-consolidate your tax position

**PSI** Polite form of 'Piss' used in front of visiting royalty or born-again Christian Americans

**REME** Indigestion tablets. Very useful, especially if Side-Salad's been using that chilli oil again

**REMFS** Rear echelon mother fucker i.e. the ones who generally stay at home i.e. most of us

**Rupert** Annoying cartoon bear with a fondness for tartan. Also any officer, though never to hi face unless his name is also Rupert

**RTU** No idea. Something to do with rugby?

**Scaley/Scaley kit** Portable Grand Prix racing set - an absolute must for long boring days hiding deep in enemy territory

**Shamag** Old tablecloth you put on your head to take the piss out of Arabs

**Shreddies** Breakfast cereal that' like a smaller, more portable version of Shredded Wheat

**Sit Rep** Tanned young blond wit a clipboard who organises day trips and only ever seems to go out with locals

**Spook** Pointed-eared know-it-all on Star Trek

**Stag** Piss-weak lager sold in Regimental bar that's so bad even the Jocks won't drink it

**Stand To** What you do when you're too blasted to stand up

**Tab** Tactical Advance with Bergens i.e. a bloody long walk in the middle of nowhere with half a house on your back

**TACBE** Sounds difficult. Avoid unless someone directly orders you to work out what it means

**VCP** Vertical Crapping Position. Not as easy as it sounds

**VIP** Very Important Postman. Take the wrong one out and thousands of grannies can wait literally months for their Christmas cards

**VPL** Nasty. Avoid by wearing loose-fitting trousers and trying not to bend down too much

# WE GIVE YOU THE POWER TO SUCCEED

## OTHER SAS PUBLICATIONS AVAILABLE FROM CASH-IN PRESS, INC.

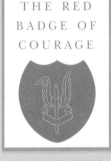

THE RED BADGE OF COURAGE

THE HEROES OF THE 1993 DILLONS BOOK-SIGNING STAMPEDE TELL THEIR STORY

IMMEDIATE TRACTION

BOOKED ON THE WRONG AIRLINE
BY ANDY MCGRABB

THE TRUE STORY OF ONE MAN'S SKIING TRIP TO THE GULF WAR

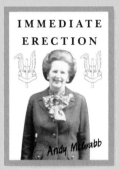

IMMEDIATE ERECTION

Andy McGrabb

AN APPRECIATION OF FORCES SWEETHEART MARGARET THATCHER

THE SAS JOKE BOOK

THE COMPLETE LIST OF SOLDIERS WHO HAVE SERVED WITH X SQUADRON

HARRY PRYCE

MACROBIOTIC PASTA DISHES UNDER FIRE

BRAVO 30 THREE ZERO

BY SGT. MELVYN BRAGG

30 YEARS OF THE SAS AMATEUR OPERATIC SOCIETY – A CELEBRATION

THE ONE THAT DIDN'T GO
BY ANDY MCGRABB

TRUE STORY OF ONE MAN'S DISAPPOINTMENT AT NOT BEING CHOSEN FOR THE BRAVO TWO ZERO MISSION

WEAPONS I HAVE SLEPT WITH

£9.99

BY GENERAL SIR PETER DE LA BILLIONÈRE

A PERSONAL MEMOIR OF THE DOOMED ROMANCE BETWEEN A VULNERABLE OFFICER AND AN AK47 WITH A DEFECTIVE SAFETY CATCH

KILLING METHODS OF THE SAS

BY THE LATE MRS ANDY MCGRABB

THEY FLEW TO PALMA

BY GENERAL SIR PETER DE LA BILLIONÈRE

X SQUADRON'S THREE-WEEK HOLIDAY IN MAJORCA WITH THE FULL LIST OF CASUALTIES

# PICTURE CREDITS